Tunguska

An Apocalyptic

Event Beyond Belief

Conrad Bauer

Copyrights

Disclaimer and Terms of Use

ISBN: 978-1533080073

Printed in the United States

Contents

Introduction

There was a huge explosion on the 30th June, 1908. Flattening 2,000 square kilometers of Siberian forest, the exact cause of the incredible blast is still unknown. Some have suggested that the event was caused by a meteor slamming into the Earth's surface. But no impact crater has ever been found. Other people have suggested that the meteor imploded in the sky above the forest. To this day, it is still the largest recorded impact event to strike the Earth. To this day, the explosion is still something of a mystery.

Thousands of scientific papers have attempted to get to the bottom of exactly what happened that day. With a force comparable to a nuclear blast, the destructive nature of the event is astounding. On the day, 80 million trees were knocked down, and the sound was heard across the continent. In the days afterwards, the night skies were lit up with odd lights. It was just the start of the strange series of events that would add a paranormal, perhaps even extraterrestrial dimension to the cataclysmic event.

Explosions such as these have the power to end all life on the planet. There's little that can be done when giant meteors rain down from above. The Tunguska Event not only demonstrates just how powerful such events can be, but also shows us what might happen if we survive. Aside from the existential threat, the fallout from the blast has left a lasting impact not just on mainstream science, but on those who dig below the surface. In this book, we will examine the explosion itself and the aftereffects that have defied explanation. Trying to figure out what caused the

Tunguska Event is one thing; trying to figure out how this explosion affected us as a planet is another matter entirely.

A Big Bang

The time was 7:14 in the morning on the 30th of June, 1908. This part of Central Siberia was deserted and free from almost all human life. Not many people wandered this far out into the wilderness, and it was a good thing they didn't. Right beside the bogs and swamps that lined the Stony Tunguska River, the world was about to change. While there might not have been a single person for miles around, the forests themselves were full of noise. Reindeer shuffled and strode through the woods, while birds sang and chirped in the treetops. The sun was out, a rare window of light for the dense Siberian territory. When the summer hit along the riverside, the mosquitos grew to ridiculous sizes. Hunting in swarms, they were dubbed flying alligators by those who would sometimes find themselves in this desolated part of the world.

The scene was almost idyllic. A perfect snapshot of the summer in Eastern Russia. And then it was gone. The sky was on fire, a blinding flash of the brightest light imaginable. A tower of fire swept through the heavens, measuring as high as an office block, hurtling towards Earth. Travelling roughly from the southeast to the northwest, the fire was bright enough as to leave a thick, burning trail in its wake, a shard of light nearly 500 miles long. It crashed through the sky at an incredible speed. Moving from the edge of human perception, it took just a few minutes for the giant, burning object to reach the ground.

But even before it hit, the world was drowned in an apocalyptic explosion. Lasting just over a second, the bang was bigger than a thousand atomic bombs. In some forty years' time, the Americans would drop an atomic bomb on the city of Hiroshima. This explosion was 1,000 times the size.

Almost instantly, over 2,000 square kilometers of the forest were flattened. The area along the banks of the Tunguska River would never be the same again. The animals were killed instantly, the birds caught with a song in their throats. The trees lay stripped and bare on the ground, seeming as though they had been felled and prepared as telegraph poles. Taking a wider view, the massive number of destroyed trees might look like someone had dropped a thousand boxes of matches all at once. Just as the silence started to return to the world, a thick mushroom of dirt and dust swelled up into the sky. It could be seen from incredible distances, the tower of smoke reaching almost eighty kilometers high. As quickly as all of the dirt, earth, and dust had been swept up, it began to rain down on the Earth once again. The crunching rainfall of the debris was the only sound to be heard in this stretch of Siberia.

This huge explosion took its name from the River at the epicenter of the destruction. The Tunguska Event, as it became known, is the single largest explosion in recorded human history. It beggars belief when attempting to comprehend the sheer scale of the damage and the strength of the blast. The event has become an obsession for some, who have tried desperately to explain how something just this destructive could ever happen and whether, importantly, it could ever happen again. For years, scientists have provided competing explanations for what happened that day. None have been able to comprehensively describe the exact events.

There are a huge number of questions that foil every scientist's attempt to explain the Tunguska Event. One of the best examples of this is the fact that no crater, crash site, or landing area has ever been found. Another is what happened to the trees, which were stripped and scattered rather than being uprooted and incinerated. No fragments of meteorites have been discovered. No eye witnesses were anywhere close to the area most affected.

Among the ideas put forward have been black holes, anti-matter, ball lightning, mirror matter, and secret government programs. But none have reached an entirely satisfying conclusion. While the most commonly accepted idea includes a giant asteroid crashing into the Earth, even this theory has its flaws. Even the aftermath of the event has allegedly left a strange influence on the area, one that is never normally discussed. During the course of this book, we will attempt to find a satisfying, scientific means of explaining the events of that fateful June morning.

Back in Tunguska on the morning on the event, the blast was starting to attract attention. Vanavara, a trading station, is located some 70 kilometers away from the affected area. A man named S. B. Semenov who lived in Vanavara remembered how he had been sitting on a chair outside his home when the force of the explosion knocked him to the ground. The air had grown so hot that his shirt almost seemed to be on fire. As he recalled, there was just a moment when he could see a "bright blue tube" lighting up the sky over an enormous area, after which everything fell dark. He lost consciousness shortly after, but he awoke moments later to find that the entire house was shaking to the point of collapse. The foundations were rumbling, and the walls shuddering. Windows were shattered, and a nearby barn collapsed. The air was still unfathomably heated, and the wind was rushing through the area, carrying dust and debris past the homes and down the streets, radiating out from the source of the explosion.

Elsewhere in Vanavara, a man named P. P. Kosolopov was walking outside his house. When the blast struck, he clapped his hands over his burning ears and tried to run back inside the building. Pieces of the ceiling were falling down and the stove blew out. The glass in his windows also shattered, while a sound like thunder echoed in the north. As soon as he could, Kosolopov stepped into the street to find everything settled after the clamor and chaos of the shockwaves.

Even to the north of Vanavara, people were affected. A small nomadic community had set up their tents in the hills, only for them to be snatched up into the air by the force of the blast. The people were left covered in bruises and confused by what had happened. One of their number, an old man, broke his arm. He had been picked up and thrown against the trunk of a tree. To another elderly member of the group, the event had been so shocking as to induce a heart attack.

The trees outside of the main site were perhaps even more affected than those close by. The event did enough to start a number of fires, which began along stretches of the treelines many miles away. These sparks grew into raging fires, and great herds of reindeer were caught in the infernos. The whole wildfire brought a thick cloud of smoke that billowed through the forest and prevented anyone from getting too close to the site.

The Tunguska River was hugely affected. Those who were fishing on boats and preparing their vessels were hit by both the blast and a rolling wave that threw them from their boats and into the air. On the banks, their horses panicked and stumbled as they tried to break free of their tethering. A further 200 kilometers away, a farmer was plowing his fields on a hillside. His horse dropped to its knees when it heard the sound of the explosion.

Remembering it sounding like gunfire, the farmer could see the trees nearby bending in half. The soil he was trying to plough was blown up around him, while he could see a huge wave racing down a nearby river. Looking to the south, he could see the pillar of fire rising up into the sky.

The force of the impact was felt hundreds of kilometers away. We can gather as much as possible about those who were near the site, but some of the more telling stories were from those who were barely in the same country. For example, the Trans-Siberian Express is the famous train that runs across Russia. As it travelled some 600 kilometers away, the carriages were shaking on the tracks, jarring passengers wildly around in their cabins. According to the driver, the tracks ahead were rippling, and so he slammed on the breaks, just in time for the thunderous sounds to reach him. Even at 700 kilometers away, people in Znamenskoye could see the bright lights rising up into the air. The sounds were audible to people in Achayevskoye, some 1,200 kilometers away, who reported hearing sounds like gunfire sounding out in the morning and lasting for a number of minutes.

But the extreme reach of the Tunguska Event was not only limited to Russia. Part of the reason why is has become so famous is because of just how global an event it became. It was indeed the largest explosion in recorded human history, heard around the globe's largest country, so it should perhaps not be a surprise to trawl through newspapers from around the world and read about strange phenomena appearing to people in distant and remote corners of the planet, people who had never heard of Tunguska until that fateful morning.

At the time, St. Petersburg was as distant from Siberia as could be. Though technically both in Russia, they were at opposite ends of the country, with the city long being held as one of the cultural links to Europe, the part of the Russian Empire that bore the strongest ties to places such as France, Great Britain, Italy, and Germany. In that regard, there was a strong interest in the nascent science of geology, and a team had set up a device to measure earthquake activity in the western Russian city. This measuring station managed to pick up the Tunguska Event despite being placed almost 4,000 kilometers away. The bang was so large that even similar stations around the planet managed to take readings for the exact same event at the exact same time.

But it was not just a physical impact left by the Event. All around the world, people were beginning to notice strange aftereffects. Of particular note were the disturbances in the Earth's magnetic field. Just like when nuclear devices are detonated, the impact on the surrounding meteorology is huge. A station in Irkutsk had been set up to take meteorological and magnetic readings and recorded a magnetic storm that lasted over four hours. When scientists poured over the data gathered about the storm, they traced the root cause all the way back to Tunguska.

Over in the United States, it would take two weeks before a similar facility in Washington D.C. recorded similarly strange happenings. The Smithsonian Astrophysical Observatory, as well as the Mount Wilson Observatory, took detailed notes of the strange decrease in the transparency of the air. Subsequent analysis has pointed towards the pillar of fire in Tunguska for causing the loss of several million tons of material burned up in the atmosphere by the singular event. In just a moment, the fireball had achieved something that it normally takes a year's worth of meteorites falling on the Earth to achieve.

As a result, there were marked changes to the skies on the nights that followed. On the evening of the Tunguska Event, people in Spain were able to gaze in awe at the bright and colorful patterns that were etched out on the dusk sky. The Astronomical Observatory in Heidelberg attempted to photograph this event, but the sheer brightness of the sky ruined their pictures. One photographer in Hamburg stepped out at 11pm to take a photograph of what he considered to be volcanic dust (recollections of the immediate aftermath of the explosion of the Krakatoa volcano in his mind). Meanwhile, those in Antwerp reported their surprise to see the skyline supposedly "on fire." Such reports were backed up by a newspaper published in Stockholm, in which these "strange illuminations" were perplexing the residents of the city.

One of the newspapers most interested in the Tunguska Events and its aftermath was the Times of London. They published a letter a few days after the event, for example, in which a reader described the "strange light" she had seen in the sky on the 1st of July, the day after the explosion. The writer, Miss Katherine Stephen, requested that someone explain the strange phenomena she had seen. The next day in the same paper, a man named Holcombe Ingleby attempted to provide a similarly perplexing observation, suggesting he had recently seen "curious sun effects." Despite the confusion as to the origin of the weird lights, they were revered as being of exquisite beauty.

At the time, news travelled slowly. Attempting to gather information about the exact happenings of the Tunguska Event in the immediate aftermath was almost impossible for a British newspaper. It is still difficult to this day, despite the technology that we now possess. The myriad claims and suggestions that appear scattered around the world's press at the time indicate the extent to which the explosion reached people, as well as the confusion it caused.

As such, it fell to the Times to attempt to supply an answer. On the 4th of July, four days after the Event itself, the newspaper admitted that similar phenomena, such as the lights in the sky, had been glimpsed across Europe. They admitted that there were many conflicting opinions about what had caused such a thing to happen. Some suggested that they were similar to the Northern Lights, the aurora borealis that is glimpsed in countries near the Arctic Circle. They also likened the events as being similar to the strange glows seen in the days following the Krakatoa eruption, admitting that there may have been an undocumented and unreported volcanic explosion elsewhere in the world. To put it simply, they did not have any idea.

In the United States, the New York Times was having an equally difficult time attempting to explain what was happening. They noted that there had been numerous reports of a yellow and white light that appeared in the sky for two nights, lasting until dawn each time. By way of an explanation, the paper suggests that "changes on the sun's surface" might be the cause of all of the strangeness. After a few days, the American paper reported claims from reporters in London and began to write about the global nature of the phenomena. As per their reports, people in London were so confused that they called the police stations and gave reports that the north of the city must be on fire.

Over the coming days, the brightness in the skies began to die down. From all over the world, from Scotland to Austria to America to Russia, reports were sent around the world as everyone attempted to figure out just what on Earth had happened. The stories were not even limited to tabloid sensationalism. Scientific journals such as Nature reported on the findings, providing data and observations to back up the strangeness but still falling short of an explanation. One of the most interesting observations came from two members of the British Association for the Advancement of Science, Mr. Shaw and Mr. Dines, who had invented an instrument known as the microbarograph. The tool was designed to measure sudden alterations in atmospheric pressure beyond what one might normally expect from a barometer. At the meeting of the Association, Mr. Shaw showed findings from six different examples of the microbarograph (each at a different location) that were taken in the hours following the Event. All of the findings showed four distinct peaks, indicating huge changes in the planet's pressure over the course of an hour. Accordingly, the scientists at the meeting put the strange findings down to a huge disturbance in the atmosphere at an as-yet-unknown location somewhere in the world.

But if the rest of the world was confused about what was happening in the night sky, then those who were much closer to the incident were not much better informed. However, the Siberian newspapers that were located much closer to the event also had more to report on. While the phenomena to reach Europe and the Americas was largely a visual one, those people who were closer to the Event knew about the full force of the explosion.

Newspapers such as Sibir in Irkutsk began to cover the story in depth. Two weeks after the Tunguska Event, they carried a story in which descriptions from villagers in Nizhne-Karelinskoye pointed towards far more than pretty lights. The stories from the people in the village indicated that there had been a huge body of white-blue light that took the form of a immense pipe. It was too bright to look at directly and began to move downwards in a vertical manner, carrying on for ten minutes before crashing into the forest. After this, a wall of black smoke began to move up and away from the crash site in every direction. The forest around was pulverized. The sound was deafening, as though large stones were falling or guns were shooting all around. Every building and home in the village began to shake. To the villagers, it seemed like the end of the world. Accordingly, they panicked.

Certain members of the Sibir's reporting team were close enough to hear the explosion themselves. One was in Kirensk, roughly 500 kilometers from the Tunguska Event. He too heard the long, drawn out sounds that echoed around the world, sounding like gunfire. He said the sounds came in bursts, a series of ten fifteen-minute periods that repeated and shattered the windows in the town's buildings.

One of the best descriptions came from the newspaper named Krasnoyarets, published in the town of Krasnoyarsk, which had a reporter stationed in Kezhma (just over 200 kilometers from the crash site.) This is the newspaper story closest to the event, the only one to come from an inhabited place that was anywhere near the explosion on the day in question. Like many of the other reports, there are descriptions of the shaking of buildings, loud noises, and general panic. However, this report not only suggests that "a subterranean shock" might be the cause, but also lists descriptions of a "heavenly body" of fire that rips through the sky from south to north. It was so big, unexpected, and quick that those who saw the body of fire could not hope to provide an exact impression. The moment that the fiery object touched the horizon, a tower of flame shot up into the air and split the sky into two. Just as soon as this vanished, then the sounds of the explosion reached the witnesses. The sound terrified the horses and cows in the village, who broke free and began to run wildly around. No one could tell where the booming sounds were originating.

This description is borne out by others from the area surrounding Tunguska. All of them seem to recall a "tongue of fire" appearing in the sky, like a beam shot through the sky and into the ground. In addition to the moment of the Event, the Siberian newspapers carried descriptions of the aftereffects. Just like the rest of the world, there were stories about the bright lights during the night and the shiny clouds that crawled across the sky. But it was difficult to collect together a definitive image of what had occurred on that day. The Russia of 1908 was vastly different from what we might have expected. Even in comparison to other Empires of the time, the Russia rulers had a number of challenges that prevented them from gathering information in the manner they might have preferred. One of our best insights into what was reported of the Tunguska Event comes from the Trading Industrial Gazette, a newspaper published in St Petersburg. On the 4th of July, 1908, they placed a small article in their paper that was titled "The Fall of the Meteorite." In the article was simply the contents of a telegram the paper had received, mentioning that though the noise had been "considerable," they were not able to confirm anything else. According to the telegrammed report, "no stone fell."

Unpicking the Russian Knot

One of the defining curiosities about the Tunguska Event is its isolation. Had it occurred in a densely populated area or even in an area close to a city of considerable size and importance, the amount of information we might have from the scene itself would be infinitely greater. However, this is tempered by the fact that surely the loss of life would have been apocalyptic should the explosion have occurred near any densely populated area. As it stands, the Tunguska Event's mystery is augmented thanks to the unique political and geographic circumstances in which it occurred. Taking place in the sparely populated backwaters of Siberia, getting to the scene, examining evidence, and making scientific conclusions was hard enough. But thanks to the particular conditions of the Russian political situation, attempting to delve deeper into the Tunguska Event became even more difficult. Because of this, the circumstances surrounding the explosion have since been mired in controversy. To better understand the Event itself, we must understand what made Russia and Siberia of the time so utterly unique.

Russia of 1908 was a powder keg waiting to explode. The political unease and the social upheaval meant that the authorities had a long list of priorities that came well before reports of an explosion in distant Siberia. Russia, even today, is the largest country in the world by landmass alone. The Russian Empire at the time was even larger but was far from the modern, mechanized states that were seen in Britain and the rest of Europe. Still ruled by a Tsar, the majority of the population was being forcibly modernized. For many centuries, Russia had clung to the model of serfdom, a slightly altered form of feudalism that meant that most people relied on agricultural work to live. With the Tsar wanting Russia to become a modern world superpower, there was a concerted effort to move away from the serf model and towards something more industrial. Contrasted against this were the ruling powers' political enemies, men and women who considered the aristocracy an outdated precept themselves and wished for them to be removed. With constant whispers about (and the occasional attempts at) revolution, it might not be a surprise to see that the Russian authorities were not concerned with pretty lights in the sky nor in muddled reports emerging from Siberia.

And this was how it would stay. Russia in the years to come would undergo more upheaval than most countries face in their entire history. Not only would the outbreak of World War I make everyone forget about the strange lights that followed the Tunguska Event, but the ensuing Bolshevik Revolution would mean the ousting of the Russian rulers as the country became the world's first communist state. With the Bolsheviks more concerned about instigating political revolution and returning the means of production to the hands of the workers, they likely had no concerns about what had happened many years earlier in Siberia. All of this meant that any research projects, groups efforts, or even desires to understand what had taken place in Siberia were pushed to the side in order to deal with the drastic changes in Russian society.

Amid the greatest social explosion in recent human history, little thought was being paid to the greatest physical explosion of all time.

Even on a smaller scale, Russian scientists and foreign thinkers began to have their heads turned in the aftermath of the Tunguska Event. Science at the time was making huge leaps and bounds on a seemingly weekly basis. As the bright lights in the sky dimmed with reports from Tunguska still confused and sparse, people's thoughts turned elsewhere. For example, Hermann Minkowski shocked the world with his theory of a fourth dimension. Ernest Rutherford presented his findings regarding the detection of the single atom. The gyroscope was invented by Herman Anschütz-Kampfe. The food additive known as MSG (monosodium glutamate) was discovered by Ikeda Kikunae. Tea bags were invented. Fuel was discovered in modern day Iran. The Zeppelin was launched. Henry Ford introduced the Model T to the world. Everywhere, it seemed, the future was arriving at an alarming rate.

Even the stranger side of science was ably covered in 1908. Reading through the newspapers at the time can furnish one with stories of everything from magnetic clouds that descended on American ships and scared the captains to ideas about alien spaceships that were racing through the sky at fantastic speeds. There was even a story from the Gulf of Mexico in which steamship passengers told lurid tales of a sea serpent that measured some 200 feet. With such outlandish tales yet to be disproven, the fog of mystery surrounding the Tunguska Event meant that it was more of a passing strangeness than an absolute obsession for many people.

There were even a number of awful natural disasters that stole headlines from Tunguska. The Messina Earthquake struck in the south of Italy and took the lives of 150,000 people. It was the most violent disaster of its type in

Europe's recorded history, with the epicenter placed right underneath the second largest city in Sicily, Messina. Alongside that, there was an international effort to combat great losses of human life, with countries agreeing upon how to send distress signals in Morse code. The SOS message is now a standard, but at the time it was a way in which people could call for help in any language. With no known causalities in Tunguska, it is probably not a surprise to see that the headlines were given to higher profile events. But, the question remains, what if the "pillar of fire" had struck the ground in London, New York, or even St Petersburg? It would be another two decades before the event really began to capture the attention of important people.

In fact, it would take two decades for more information to reach the Western world. The Tunguska Event (as it later became known) had been all but forgotten about by 1928, World War I doing more than enough to shift the strange lights from the planet's memory. It took twenty years for the stories about the giant fireball to dribble through to western thinkers and another year before a British astronomer named C. J. P. Cave examined the news stories about the fireball and compared them to the atmospheric data taken from the microbarographs around Britain. When he pointed out the consistencies between dates and times of the fluctuations and the strange legends of the fire pillar, other scientists began to take notice.

Among them was Fred Whipple, an American astronomer who would later find fame for his modelling of comets known as the "dirty snowball" theory. According to Whipple, the airwaves in England were directly affected by events in Tunguska, which became known (rightly or wrongly) as the Siberian Meteorite. The American announced his thoughts that the strange microbarograph readings were not linked to the Siberian events at the time, describing the Tunguska Event as "a story without parallel in historical times." He then remarked how odd it was that the event was so "nearly ignored." Taking the information gathered from the microbarographs, Whipple was able to show that the pressure fronts caused by the Tunguska Event were travelling around the world at a speed of over 1,000 kilometers an hour, similar to those that had been seen in the wake of the Krakatoa explosion. The findings, as he interpreted them, seemed to point to the first four waves being caused when a giant meteorite entered into the Earth's atmosphere, with a final couple of waves resulting from said meteorite's impact into the ground.

The paper was published, and the world began to take notice.

The research was taken up by Spencer Russell, a fellow astronomer, who was one of the first in the west to link the explosion with the strange lights seen in the sky. After twenty years, there was finally the inklings of a proper investigation (at least, one outside of Russia) into what might have happened that day. But while the events and the phenomena were being linked by the scientists, the ideas that they were putting forward were based on speculation. The focus seemed to be on explaining the bright lights and the strange instrument readings, but the Tunguska Event was so much more. Despite the wealth of knowledge at the disposal of the Western world, there was an acceptance to positing theories without a full set of information. What had happened in Russia, it seemed, was the business of the Russians. And so it fell to a young

Russian to conduct a full investigation. Out of view of the rest of the world and under the cloak of the newly formed Soviet state, one scientist began to try to peel away the mysteries of the Tunguska Event.

The Bolshevik Revolution of 1917 completely altered the way in which the country was organized. So complete were the changes to the country that it would be five years before they settled on a new name for themselves: the Union of Soviet Socialist Republics, otherwise known as the USSR. In the aftermath of the revolution, there was a distinct need for money. Having overthrown the Tsar, and with World War I having ended without their participation, the entire world was watching on with concern as a new specter began to haunt Europe and beyond: the idea of international communism.

But one of the best hopes of money for the newly formed country lay in news from the capitalist West. In America, there was a growing excitement around the idea of iron. Not just any iron, this was iron (as well as other metals) that might be extracted from the ground. While many metals come from ores that have long been buried in the Earth's surface, these new substances had a decidedly more extraterrestrial lineage. The clamor surrounding the idea of the meteorite meant that there might be huge amounts of mineral wealth just lurking beneath the world's surface. In a country desperate to industrialize, a massive source of iron would be hugely welcome and very financially rewarding.

Amid these rumors of space riches lurking beneath the soil, the people of Russia suddenly remembered the Tunguska Event. At that point, the strange goings-on of 1908 had become something of a footnote in the country's recent history. But the idea that there might be iron buried deep beneath Siberia seemed almost too tantalizing. So it fell to a young scientist named Leonid Alekseyevich Kulik to uncover the truth about what had happened that day.

As you might expect, the events that had occurred in 1908 – having been ignored by the scientific community for so long – had trickled into local folklore. For those who lived in the small villages and towns within a few hundred miles of Tunguska, the event seemed like a mix between a warning from God and the end of the world as they knew it. It might have been the testing of a new super weapon by the government a thousand miles away or an attack from some foreign superpower that wished ill on Mother Russia. Among those more in tune with the science fiction literature of the day, the possibility that the event had alien origins was something to be considered. But, essentially, every story told was based on scurrilous rumors, hand-me-down stories, and ancient mythologies crafted together to explain the inexplicable.

But aside from this folklore, Leonid was a scientist. His background as a mineralogist and a specialist on all matters concerning meteorites meant that he was a natural choice for the expedition to the heart of Tunguska. In his opinion, the Event was exactly in line with his specialties. A meteorite – one of tremendous size – must have struck the area concerned. Over a period between 1927 and 1939, he made four trips to the site in order to attempt to prove his theory. But there was only one problem: whenever he went, wherever he looked, Leonid could not find any remains of the meteorite. If his theory was to be true, a meteorite larger than any in recorded history should be buried beneath the soil. But there was nothing to be found.

The chief pursuit, in order to track down the riches of metal beneath the surface, was the crater. If a giant object had struck the Earth, as the stories seemed to suggest, then it seemed logical to Leonid that there should be a point of impact. As this point of impact, there should be a large crater left behind. There are other spots around the world where confirmed meteorite strikes have taken place, such as the Chicxulub crater in Mexico. The Mexican site features a huge raised circle, exactly as you might imagine would be left behind by an impact measured on a global scale. But Leonid found nothing.

The question haunted the scientist. He had been an excellent scholar since his earliest days. This came to an end when he was expelled for his involvement with the Bolshevik party, an act of expulsion that served him only too well when the Bolsheviks came to power. Studying under Vladimir Vernadsky in the Ural Mountains, he transformed from a politically minded student into a field-leading scientist. His grasp of minerology was prodigious, and he soon outgrew the Ural posting. He was given his own expedition, leading a team dispatched from St Petersburg University. After a brief pause in which he was conscripted into the Army as part of World War I, he resumed his studies, this time with the Army. Following the October Revolution, he took a teaching position at Tomsk University, before eventually returning to St Petersburg. At the time, the study of meteorites was a relatively new field, but he quickly distinguished himself among his peers.

It was no shock when he was chosen by the Soviet Academy of Sciences to lead the first expedition to find meteorites in 1921. Before searching Tunguska, the group was tasked with tracking down space debris nearer inhabited areas. When this expedition first set out, it seemed that Leonid was entirely unaware of the Tunguska incident. Indeed, it seems that the Tunguska Event first reached him when he was about to set off on their trip. Just as the train was about to pull away from the station, an editor of a scientific magazine ran on to the platform and handed Leonid a clipping from a calendar published in 1910. The clipping featured one of the first speculations that a meteorite might have fallen near Kansk. In the ensuring events, everyone seemed to have forgotten about it. But furthermore, the calendar clipping told a story of how a train driver and his crew had come across the meteorite itself, lying red hot and cooling on the ground when they had been forced to stop. It was entirely buried in the ground, but thought to measure almost 14 meters across. Even to a famed meteorite specialist such as Leonid, the story was entirely new. It became an obsession.

The idea burrowed into Leonid's mind and refused to let go. Several stops were made in places such as Omsk, Tomsk, and Krasnoyarsk, but it was not until they eventually reached Kansk that Leonid and his team were able to take their ideas and investigate further. The Siberian newspapers were one of their first points of interest, and they scanned the pages from 1908 to find out more. On closer inspection, Leonid found the source of the item from the calendar, but was dismayed to find that it was almost entirely incorrect. Nevertheless, the stories about the existence of a giant meteorite in Kansk seemed to be true. The stories were everywhere. To get to the bottom of the problem, Leonid prepared a questionnaire to be taken by the local people. He published two and a half thousand copies and handed them out. The accounts that came back to him, though separated by more than a decade from the event, were rich and detailed. Gathering together the wealth of information, Leonid even managed to paint a picture of what he deemed the Filimonovo Meteorite.

By this point, Leonid was convinced that there had been a meteorite strike on the 30th of June, 1908. The moment he returned from his expedition, he submitted a paper to the Academy in which he outlined his beliefs. Inside the report was the demand that he and his team simply must investigate further. Despite publishing his findings, the Academy remained skeptical. But Leonid had backup. Director of the Irkutsk Magnetic and Meteorological Observatory, A.V. Voznesensky, reinforced the claimed by pointing to the air and seismic waves that had been recorded at the time, suggesting that they could only have been caused by a giant object such as a meteorite. But Voznesensky's report differed slightly. Instead of impacting the Earth, he wondered whether the meteorite might have exploded some 30 kilometers above the surface. Between Leonid and Voznesensky, there was an absolute conviction that something had fallen from the sky that day.

In order to ratify his claims, Voznesensky pointed towards a belief held by the Native Americans of Arizona. In the state of Arizona is a large crater that has been verifiably caused by a meteorite strike, but that was written into legend as the fiery chariot that crashed out of the sky. The people who lived in the vicinity passed down the legend from one generation to the next, and it was only recently that scientific investigations had been able to suggest that the stories were more than just folklore. Rather than being just a myth, the burning chariot was rooted in the incredibly destructive interstellar object that crashed into the planet. If the Tunguska Event was anything similar, Voznesensky suggested, then a search for the meteorite could prove to be incredibly lucrative.

Accounts came from beyond the scope of the traditional sciences, as well. An ethnographer named I. M. Suslov published a report in 1926 that investigated the eyewitness accounts from the time of the huge explosion. Taking in the stories of 60 people, Suslov was able to point towards the repeated use of phrases and expressions. These included the ideas that the forest had been crushed and the reindeer annihilated, that the stores of grain had been wiped out and many people were injured. Even across a large number of witness statements, the same images cropped up again and again. They all seemed to point towards the existence of a huge meteorite that had crashed into the Earth. With the overwhelming amount of evidence pointing towards the existence of such a potentially rewarding object, the Academy seemed to have no other option than to sanction another expedition for Leonid.

The first expedition set out in February of 1927. By this time, St Petersburg had been renamed to Leningrad, from which Leonid departed with just one assistant. They took the railway, the Trans-Siberian network being the quickest way to get across the country. By the 12th of February, they had reached Taishet, a station located around 900 kilometers south of the main site of the Tunguska Event. They prepared by purchasing food and other supplies, knowing that they would have to make the rest of the journey in a more difficult manner. With their horse-drawn sleighs, the pair battled against regular snowstorms and freezing temperatures. By the time they reached Kezhma, they had travelled to within 215 kilometers of the site in five days. Here, they stocked up, refreshed their horses, and set off again on the 22nd of March.

The Siberian winter was (and still is) a bitter foe. The snow was thick, and it made travel difficult, while the cold bore down on the travelers every single second. The terrain was tough, with creeks, swamps, bogs, and mountainsides all hidden amongst the dense snow. At certain times, the duo was forced to cross rivers by taking huge detours, simply because the supposed bridges were too dangerous to cross. The forest around Siberia has claimed many lives and is rightly regarded as one of the most dangerous places in the world. It took Leonid and his assistant three days to arrive in Vanavara, which was the closest thing to civilization to be found near their destination.

By way of an introduction, Leonid had been given a letter to hand over to the local Soviet political officer. It requested that the holder be put in touch with a local man named Ilya Potapovich, a member of the Evenki population that lives in the region. When introduced, however, Potapovich flatly declined to offer any help, especially in reaching what the Evenki described as the home of the Thunder God. To them, the land was both forbidden and sacred. The Tunguska Event, to the Evenki people, had been a visit from their god of thunder, Ogdy, with the smashing of trees and killing of animals being a curse wrought upon the area. It took a great deal of persuading for Leonid to convince the local man, but in the end, a hefty bribe seemed convincing enough. Potapovich would take them, but it would cost several spools of cloths, a couple of bags of flour, and building materials enough to repair the floor and the roof of Potapovich's home.

Now with a local guide, Leonid was determined to reach the site as soon as possible. He attempted to set off immediately, but the poor weather and the fatigue of the horses meant that they were forced to turn around and wait for the weather to clear. It would be the 8th of April before the conditions were right, and they set off with enough supplies to last them a month. While waiting for the weather to clear, they had acquired a second guide. Okhchen was also an Evenki man, and it was his hut they reached after 40 kilometers of travel.

Swapping their horses for reindeer, they began to follow the Chamba River deeper and deeper into the forest. After another two days of travelling, they reached the end of the path. By this time, they had been travelling through the terrible conditions for five days, and it had taken a huge toll. The men were exhausted and seemed to have contracted scurvy, as well as a number of other infections, thanks to their particularly poor and restricted diet. But Leonid was more determined than ever. They took their axes and began to hack through the undergrowth.

On the 13th of April, the group had their first sight of the fallen trees. They seemed as though they had been ripped from the ground by some great force and were still lying in the same position many years later. Two days later, when climbing up the Shakrama Mountain, Leonid looked out over the site of the explosion. Standing behind him, Potapovich informed him that this was the spot where the god had rained down thunder and lightning on the world.

The sight from the top of the mountain was breathtaking. There was a 70 kilometer wide plateau in an almost oval shape. It was a patch in which the entire forest had been flattened. All of the trees lay stripped and bare, fallen away from the direct epicenter of the blast. Even from up high, it was possible to see that the huge trees had been snapped like twigs. Whatever had done this had been an incredibly powerful force. It was no surprise that the Evenki people had attributed the work to a god.

But Leonid was not content to stand up high and appreciate the view. He wanted to be right down in the center of the plateau. If he was to find the meteorite itself, then it must surely be right in the middle? It must have been driven into the Earth at the point in the center of all the felled trees. The true center of the blast, where the trees had not been felled so much as entirely obliterated, lay to the north. They were closer than ever to ground zero of the Tunguska Event, but they would go no further. Despite Leonid's protestations, the guide refused to enter into the area that had so clearly been cursed by their god. Distraught and furious, Leonid had no choice but to pack up and travel back to Vanavara.

Leonid expanded his party and brought in locals from neighboring villages. He was determined to find the point of impact and to discover the huge amounts of iron that had surely been left behind. His new expedition left on the 30th of April, travelling deeper into the Siberian forest, aided by the thawing winter snow. Reaching a part of the area named the South Swamp by the Evenki people, he could see new levels of destruction. Despite the many years that had passed, it was clear just how powerful the Tunguska Event had been. To Leonid, he seemed to be in the belly of some great cauldron, and he was convinced that this was the epicenter that he had been searching for. For 30 kilometers in every direction, the forest amounted to piles of stripped trees that looked exactly like telegraph poles. Occasionally, a tree might be left standing, but every branch and twig had been ripped away to leave only a desolate silhouette standing up among the pile of poles. Writing in his diary, Leonid mentioned that the area had been "completely flattened." The trees still lay in the direction that they had been blown down. All across the great cauldron, their angles were slightly different. Each fallen tree seemed to radiate out from some central point. This, thought Leonid, must be the point of impact.

The area was cold and dead. The fallen trees dominated the landscape, and many clearly displayed signs of having been caught in a fire. Unlike usual forest fires, these scorch marks did not linger around the bottom of the trees, but uniformly marked them. It was as though a massive wave of heat had washed over them all at once. For the men new to the area, it was almost like an alien wasteland, unlike anything else in the world.

But there was hope. On closer inspection, Leonid could find traces of growth and plant life, signs that life might be returning to the area. Even though the trees that had fallen down represented many decades worth of life, there seemed to be indications that – ever since the aftermath of the Tunguska Event had died down – vegetation was working its way back into the area. But this was of no concern to the scientist. He was tasked with finding a meteorite, not with documenting biological life.

One point of interest were the large circular ridges that rose up. They were almost like ripples in water, but they were formed by the solid ground. It might be that these had been formed when the object struck the Earth and forced the ground to move outwards. It was a giant version of dropping a pebble into a pile of dense mud. But rather than finding evidence of one giant crater as can be seen in other places around the world, Leonid was shocked to discover that there were instead many smaller versions scattered around the forest. There seemed to be dozens of the smaller entities, which he likened to "lunar craters," which ranged from 10 to 50 meters in diameter and could be up to four meters deep. Though the edges were steep, their basins were filled with a flat and swampy mud.

Annoyed that he had not found the traces of the giant meteorite as expected, Leonid was forced to return once again to Vanavara. His team were running out of food, and the journey was long and treacherous. He arrived back in the town towards the end of June before departing back to Leningrad. Needing to submit a report to the Academy, he included pictures of the shallow craters that he had found, suggesting that they hinted towards the small fragments of a much larger object that remained hidden. Taking measurements, these larger craters could belong to meteorites weighing around 130 tons each and were, in all probability, made of iron. Having fallen on the territory of the Soviet Union, Leonid implored his superiors that they were duty-bound to explore the area.

In response, the Academy seemed to agree. They approved a second expedition to Tunguska, though allocated only enough funds to map the area and to take magnetic readings. Leonid was also tasked with the mission of collecting meteorite fragments to bring back to the museum headquarters. By this point, the investigations had even attracted interest from the Western newspapers. A number of publications ran stories describing the possibility of a meteorite being behind the Tunguska Event, but focused their attentions on the question of what might have happened had the object struck a built-up area. With interest growing about the Tunguska Event, but budgets slashed, Leonid was under increasing pressure to find the traces of his meteorite.

This time, Leonid's team was different. Setting off in April of 1928, he had with him a man named V Sytin, his assistant, who was a specialist in hunting and zoology. By the time they reached Vanavara, they were joined by N. A. Strukov, a cinematographer. At first, their progress was delayed by floods in the region, and it was not until June that they reached the site. First, the entire area of 100 square kilometers was surveyed and documented in order to make future expeditions easier. Leonid attempted to dig down into the base of some of the craters, but his progress was halted by the swampy mud in the bottom which made digging impossible. Without water pumps to drain the craters, he was stuck. Furthermore, the basic tools he had for measuring magnetic fields were failing to register anything of note, unable to detect anything interesting.

Strukov took a number of reels of film of the site, including footage of the scientists hard at work, but he left after a few weeks. Leonid and three people were left behind, collecting samples and plant materials. By the time August rolled around, members of the team were again exhibiting signs of vitamin deficiency, and the money was starting to run out. Any prospect of finding the meteorite itself was growing increasingly slim. Should he return to the Academy with no proof, then future funding would surely be hard to come by. So Leonid devised a plan. He sent back two of his workers, who would travel to the Academy and appeal for more funding while he stayed behind on the site.

At this point, Leonid received a massive stroke of luck. As Sytin arrived back in Moscow to talk to the Academy, the papers were full of a story that captured the nation's rapturous attention. An airship named the Italia had crash landed in the Arctic, and Soviet crews had risked their lives to recover the people. When Sytin brought back news of another Russian risking his life out in the wilderness for the greater glory of the USSR, the Academy found themselves under great pressure to allocate more funds. They sanctioned both a rescue operation and a renewed investigation into the Tunguska Event. This allowed them to continue through to October, by which time they returned to Vanavara and then on to Leningrad.

By this time, Leonid had become something of a celebrity. Not only had his story become famous in Russian, but the film shot by Strukov – titled *In Search of the Tunguska Meteorite* – had been released to wide acclaim. His expeditions had even been reported in Britain and America. The New York Times went as far as to value the discovery of the meteorite at $1,000,000, a huge sum at the time. The Literary Digest went a step further and published a comment from Sytin that valued the metals – iron and platinum – at something like $100,000,000. But, he stated, it was not just the financial rewards but also the scientific benefits that appealed to the men searching for the meteorite. Under a cloud of celebrity, Leonid began to prepare for his third expedition.

The third journey into Tunguska was much bigger. Lasting from February in 1929 through to October in 1930, it included many more scientists and a renewed commitment to discovering the truth behind the Tunguska Event. As an example of just how much bigger an operation this was, the team took with them horses dragging fifty carts. These fifty carts contained drilling machines, surveying instruments, and water pumps, everything the scientists might need to document every single inch of the explosion site.

Leonid had become convinced in his theory that the largest crater – that he had named after Suslov – and the surrounding smaller craters were the result of the falling of separate pieces of the meteor. So he decided to dig down into the basin. Leonid and his team dug four meters down into the Suslov crater, a process that took them an entire month. Their excavations revealed no "impact features," however, with the team only managing to uncover a decaying tree stump. It seemed as though the famed Suslov crater was nothing more than a natural landscape formation.

The scientists began to bicker and squabble about the location of the epicenter of the Event. Krinov, having surveyed the area independently, suggested that the crash site might be further to the south. Leonid was furious and banished him from the expedition. Leonid was convinced by the importance of the Suslov crater and told his team to set up the drilling rig. They drilled a hole to the depth of 34 meters, measuring four meters wide, an astonishingly difficult feat in the frozen grounds of the Siberian tundra. But still there was no meteorite fragments to be found. After a few more holes were drilled into the ground, Leonid finally gave up on his hypothesis on the 1st of March, 1930. At last, he conceded that the Suslov crater was nothing more than an interesting piece of the landscape.

By the time he returned to Leningrad, six months had passed and Leonid appeared "with grey hair" and "ruined health." It seemed as though the third, larger expedition had taken a great toll on the man. Indeed, it would be almost a decade before he was able to return to the site of his obsession. The time allowed him to reflect and recuperate, even going so far as to apologize to Krinov. Because, by this point, Leonid had realized that he was wrong. By now, he too believed that the true impact area was to be found in the south, in the area that the Evenki named the South Swamp.

One of the greatest leaps forward in the Soviets' understanding of the Tunguska region came in 1938. Thanks to the advances in aircraft technology, it became possible to conduct an aerial survey of the area. With these photographs, scientists finally had an overhead way of looking at the strange radial nature of the trees as they had fallen. Lying at the heart of the blast, as it now seemed, was the South Swamp. Setting off in 1939, Leonid once again headed up an expedition to Tunguska. The intention was to drill in the areas around the south parts of the great cauldron. These drillings gave the scientists an idea of the cavities that existed below the surface of the Earth. While some scientists pointed out that these were natural formations, Leonid figured them to be underground craters and thus proof that this was the area he had been searching for all the long. The Academy sided with him once again and agreed to a fifth expedition to take place in 1940.

However, this fifth expedition would never take place. Once again, the apocalyptic geopolitics of the world distracted the Russians from uncovering the truth about Tunguska. The outbreak of World War II meant that any thoughts of trips to Siberian swamps were quickly dismissed. Indeed, Operation Barbosa was launched on the 5th of July, 1941, with Nazi Germany attacking the Soviet Union. Leonid, formerly an Army man himself, joined the cause. Fighting on the Eastern front, he took a wound to the leg and was then captured by German troops in October of that year. Shipped to the prisoner camp in Spas-Demensk, he stayed imprisoned until he died. Contracting typhus, Leonid Alekseyevich Kulik passed away on the 14th of April, 1942, at the age of 58. Eventually, Leonid would have a street in Vanavara, an asteroid, and even a crater on the Moon all named after him.

The war finished in 1945, but renewed interest in the Tunguska Event was not rekindled until 1958. Without the obsessed efforts of Leonid dictating the interests of the Academy in St Petersburg, many other projects took precedent. Among them were the developments of nuclear weapons and efforts to put men into space.

However, after the initial expeditions in 1958, interest began to grow. By 1963, as many as 29 investigations were sanctioned by the Academy of Sciences. By 1989, even foreign scientists had been invited to the site to attempt to provide answers. In the current day, a 4,000 square kilometer region surrounding Tunguska has been designated as a national reserve, keeping it free of interference. But that is not to say the site itself was any more accessible. The nearest railway station on the

Trans-Siberian Express was still some 600 kilometers away from Vanavara. Since the 1930s, this small town had swelled and was now home to more than 4,000 people. To reach the site of the Tunguska Event, you had to either hike or charter a helicopter.

But despite this, there was still no adequate explanation for the Tunguska explosion. No evidence of a buried meteorite had ever been found at the site, despite the clues pointing towards Leonid's grand cauldron as being the only logical location. When surveying Tunguska, this was the only point that seems logical for something so cataclysmic to have taken place. The local Evenki people had enshrined the spot in their folklore. The seismic waves ripple out from an obvious epicenter. The fallen trees seemed to stem outwards from one significant point. But there was nothing buried beneath the Earth.

Writing on the subject later, Krinov proposed another theory. According to his beliefs, the meteorite did not drive itself deep into the Earth. Instead, it exploded high above the area, above Leonid's great cauldron. But Krinov himself has no evidence beyond hypothesizing. Other theories put forward have included comets, miniature black holes, anti-matter, asteroids, or a methane gas explosion rising up from deep inside the Earth. There had even been suggestions centered on alien landing craft and conspiratorial weapons testing. Some had even put forward the theory that there may have been a laser beam shot directly into the planet by extraterrestrial life. Whether this was an attempt to communicate or an act of aggression, the theory did not say. But all of these suggestions lacked the single most important quality: evidence. As we look deeper into the mysteries of the Tunguska Event in the coming chapters, you will see why trying to piece together proof proves to be so very difficult indeed.

The Peculiarity of Tunguska

The Tunguska Event is one of the strangest things to have happened in recorded human history. The bizarre blend of complete and utter destructive power and the relative isolation of the explosion site have meant that the theories of what actually happened have devolved into guesswork. There are many competing explanations, and not all are simple. While many people ascribe to the idea of a huge meteorite, others have journeyed deeper into the Siberian wilderness and tried to make sense of what they found. Perhaps because of the inexplicable nature of the Tunguska Event, it is impossible to dismiss even the most far-fetched theory. For many people, the obsession with the explosion can only be satiated by looking at the stranger explanations. Before we wander into the mainstream, what are the more mysterious explanations for the Tunguska Event?

A Strange Ship

To understand the first theory in this chapter, we will need to travel back to 1945. Almost four decades after the Tunguska Event, August of that year was the first time in which humanity as a species came anything close to replicating an explosion of that magnitude. The culprits were Little Boy and Fat Man. These were the names given to the bombs dropped on Hiroshima and Nagasaki respectively. The first fell on the 6th of August, while the second followed three days later. To this day, they have been the only examples of a nuclear device used in an act of aggression.

One of the best descriptions we have of the event comes from the Pilot of the B-29 that flew over Hiroshima. For obvious reasons, first-hand accounts from the ground are hard to come by, but Colonel Paul Tibbets' account provides a unique perspective. He was speaking at a press conference following the dropping of the bomb, laying out to journalists the sight he saw beneath him. According to Tibbets' account, there was a "tremendous black cloud" rising up and up with incredible speed. The place where the city had been just seconds before was now replaced entirely by a "mountain of smoke." In that smoke, the pilot could see a twenty-thousand-foot-high mushroom made entirely of boiling dust. This same scene continued for around three or four minutes while the crew watched. Then, from the center of the cloud, a white plume began to appear and rose up to twice the height. Now further away, they could see the edges of the city, where a number of fires had broken out. Buildings had begun to crumble and collapse while gas mains caught fire and exploded. Paul Tibbets flew back to base.

There were some people who were able to provide accounts from the ground, however. A memorable testimony comes from Kiyosi Tenimoto, who was a church pastor for the Hiroshima Methodist group. The church was about four kilometers from the place where the bomb dropped, just far enough away to not be atomized. What he described was a flash of light so bright as to be blinding. As soon as it arrived, the "sheet of sun" was replaced by the appearance of a colossal mushroom cloud, the same sight that we now come to associate with the detonation of an atomic bomb.

These accounts were backed up by John Hersey, a journalist working for the New York Times, who was able to visit the bomb sites in the immediate aftermath of the detonation. According to his interviews with witnesses from the surrounding areas, the blasts had appeared as a "noiseless flash of light," and there were very few people who could actually remember hearing the sound of the bombs exploding. To them, it was first a blinding light, followed by an intense feeling of heat, then the incredible din of the explosion, and the shock that it brought with it. Hersey's accounts were collected together and published into a book at the same time as they were published in the newspaper, becoming a key part of people's understandings of the power of the atomic bomb.

Indeed, one need only look at the raw numbers to understand just how potent these devices were. At the center of the blast, the temperature of the air was raised to a million degrees Celsius. The 15 kiloton atomic bombs were both detonated some 600 meters above the ground, exploding before they hit the Earth. The surface directly below where they exploded recorded temperatures of around 6,000 degrees Celsius. In their wake, the bombs left behind an orange mushroom-shaped cloud that rose to ten kilometers. The cloud itself could wreak huge amounts of damage, starting fires that are reported to have killed as many as 140,000 Japanese people and damaging around 70,000 houses. There were even more deaths in the aftermath thanks to the radiation sickness that lingered on at the sites. This is reported to have killed close to 200,000 men, women, and children. In just a few short minutes, around 340,000 people were wiped out by a single atomic device.

As a species, we now know just how terrible the destructive power of the atomic bomb can be. The combination of the giant fireball, the deadly mushroom cloud, and the incinerating heat all combine to provide humanity with one of its most deadly weapons. In the aftermath of the detonation of the two devices in Japan, it was not long before writers in the Soviet Union and beyond began to include the images from Nagasaki and Hiroshima in their works. It was only a little longer still before these images were linked with the Tunguska Event. Just like the atomic bombs, the aftermath of the explosion in Siberia had included tales of a huge fireball, a destructive cloud, and heat that left trees burned and tossed out of the way as though they were mere twigs.

One of the foremost writers in this regard was a man named Alexander Kazantsev. Once an engineer who had graduated from Siberia's technical institute in 1930, he was the author of a soon-to-be-famous short story named *Vokrug Sveta* or *The Blast*. Published in 1946, the story appeared in one of the USSR's best-selling science and adventure magazines. As part of the plot, Kazantsev put forward the idea that the Tunguska Event was caused by what he described as a "cosmic visitor." This was, ostensibly, a UFO. As he saw it, it would be in the shape of a cylinder and powered by nuclear fuel. Having suffered from a malfunction, the ship had hurtled towards Earth and had crashed in Tunguska. The ship and every being aboard was vaporized. The story suggested that the pilots of the craft had been hoping to travel to Lake Baikal, some 800 kilometers from the crash site, home to the world's deepest body of freshwater.

The story was well-received, and the hypothesis of the alien visitors causing the Tunguska Event became well-known and well-used by other writers. As more and more findings were sent back from the location by the Academy of Sciences, writers began to incorporate these findings into the stories. Kazantsev himself reworked *The Blast* a number of times based on the updated research. When the 1958 expedition told of discoveries of metals such as cobalt, copper, and nickel, the author adjusted the story to explain their presence. After some time, the theory of what had happened – at least according to the writer – began to grow more and more complete. For example, the discovery of nickel and cobalt were explained as being the metals used in the hull of alien spacecraft. Germanium and copper, meanwhile, were the substances used by the conductors in the UFO. They had all been vaporized when the ship exploded and had fallen to Earth for the scientists to discover at a later date.

Despite the popularity of the books, not everyone was impressed. The Soviet Astronomical Journal widely criticized the books, claiming that they deceived the reader on a "consistent and conscious" basis. According to their criticisms, Kazantsev had one purpose, which was to demonstrate that he and only he knew the truth about the Tunguska Event, a truth that ran contrary to all of the available evidence. That's not to say that every scientist was against the author. A. Y. Manotskov, an aircraft designer, was a known adherent to Kazantsev's theories and believed that the object that had caused the Tunguska Event must have been under "intelligent control." As evidence, he proposed that the majority of comets and meteorites enter the Earth's atmosphere at speeds of between 36 and 216 thousand kilometers an hour. In the case of the Tunguska event, however, the object had (according to Manotskov) "braked" down to around 2,400 kilometers per hour, a comparable speed to a fighter jet. If the object had been a meteorite, he proposed, then it would have needed to have a mass of at least 1 billion tons and a diameter of just over a kilometer. But there were no fragments left behind, not even an impact crater. According to Manotskov (and Kazantsev agreed), the object must have been a spaceship. Boris Laipunov, one of the Soviets' best known space and rocket experts, seemed to agree with the pair.

But there was more reasoning to come. Feliks Zigel, who worked for the Moscow Aviation Institute, added further weight to the claims that the object had been under "intelligent control." Taking a number of eyewitness accounts, he suggested that the flight path of the object had twice changed its course when moving through the sky. These accounts, however, had been taken long after the Event and were doubted by some. For Zigel, however, they were only further proof. To him, this kind of controlled descent was evidence of the object being a spaceship, its owners piloting it before the explosion. But his proof went even further. According to figures he presented, the supposed ship performed a massive loop, the kind of loop that would preclude a natural flight path. The re-entry angle of the spaceship, Zigel suggested, was exactly 6.2 degrees. This is within the re-entry corridor that cosmonauts and other human space travelers use when returning to Earth. Enter too steeply and the ship burns up, enter too shallow and the ship will simply bounce off the atmosphere and back into space. Thanks to the angle of the supposed spacecraft seen over Tunguska, Zigel believed that the pilots knew exactly what they were doing.

Zigel has been described by some as the originator of Ufology in the USSR. Perhaps that is why he took so many opportunities to praise Kazantsev's observations and to declare them to be true. In 1959, he went as far as to opine that it was the only realistic theory yet to be suggested. It explained both the lack of a suitable crater and the large explosion witnessed by so many people. In his opinion, the more information and research that was conducted regarding the Tunguska Event, the more and more likely it became that the explosion was the result of an incident aboard an alien probe. To the State, however, such allegations were an annoyance. The national newspaper of the Soviet Union, Pravda, considered speculation about UFOs to be an entirely America construction. Locked in an ideological Cold War with the United States, the Soviets had sometimes suggested that the idea of little green men in flying saucers were planted in their public by the Pentagon. Despite the writers' attempts to explain the Tunguska Event, the authorities tried to ignore them. While this might have been possible in Russia, thoughts of alien interference on Earth were not just confined to Siberia.

An American Import

It seems far-fetched and obtuse to pin the events in Tunguska as being the work of extraterrestrial life. It takes a huge leap to go from scientific investigations into known phenomena such as meteorites to those subjects usually treated with derision. It doesn't help that the Soviet Union's most vocal endorsers of the theory were authors rather than the cadre of researchers and scientists on the ground. But the dismissal of the UFO theory as an American import or propaganda tool does it a disservice. Indeed, similar theories had arisen outside of the knowledge of the Tunguska Event, entirely independently. One of the most famous of these occurred in 1947, in a town in New Mexico that would soon become infamous.

It was the 8th of July when the story broke in the Roswell Daily Record. There were stories of a strange interaction that had happened in New Mexico, with the headline stating that the RAAF (Roswell Army Air Field) had actually managed to capture a real life flying saucer on a nearby ranch. The RAAF was situated near the ranch of Mac Brazel, who reared sheep. His lands were some 140 kilometers to the west of the town of Roswell, and one night when he was out and about, he happened to come across a pile of wreckage. To him, it seemed as though it was made of rubber, wood, plastic, tape, and tinfoil. There were strange markings on the debris, which the rancher compared to hieroglyphics. It was very unusual, something the likes of which he had never seen before. It was a few days before Brazel could drive into town, but when he did he informed the local Sheriff. The Sheriff, in turn, reported the find to an Intelligence Officer named Major Jesse Marcel at the nearby base.

It was not long before the Army was on the scene and closing off the site to the public. The wreckage was still there but was being cleared. To the officers, there were rumors and rumblings that this was an authentic flying saucer. While the wreckage was shipped off to be examined by someone better qualified, the Commander at the Army base decided to release a press statement in which he confirmed the recovery of the wreckage of a flying saucer.

Within no time at all, the story was on the front page of every newspaper. But the sensation was to be cut short. After just a few hours, the press were recalled to the offices of the man who had conducted the examination and were told that the news had been a case of mistaken identity. The wreckage had in fact belonged to a weather balloon. The next day, the Roswell Daily Record reported the deflated story, correcting the version of events to the official one given out by the government.

But there was more to the story. There were rumors circulating around the town of Roswell that originated with the people who had seen the actual wreckage. Though these were never printed, it became a commonly held truth in the town that there had been "bodies" found near the scene of the accident and they were not human. Described as measuring roughly one meter tall, possessing a bluish tint to the hairless skin, and with no hair or ears, these little men were explained away by the authorities as being crash dummies that were dropped from the balloon in order to measure impact. And so the town was led to believe. For years, that was the story that stuck, even if a number of people were not convinced.

One of those people who was not convinced went on to write a book. Published in 1980, *The Roswell Incident* was one of the first to put into print the tales and rumors that had circulated among certain groups about what had really happened in Roswell. The writer concluded that there had been a massive cover-up to hide the truth about the wreckage that was discovered. This was followed in 1988 by another book, *UFO Crash at Roswell*, which was even more explicit in its claim that the United States government had covered up the recovery of alien lifeforms in Roswell. Many of the conspiratorial claims put forward regarding the United States' involvement in the alien cover-ups can be traced to this incident and to these books. The truth, whatever you believe, is likely far more benign and boring. But for many people, the possibility that we are not alone in the universe is almost taken as gospel.

Even the term UFO (standing for Unidentified Flying Object) was originally invented by the United States Air Force. Put forward in the 1950s, it was thought to be a better fit that the phrase "flying saucer," seeing as many of the reported incidents could be explained by natural forces. While the U in UFO does stand for unidentified, this does not necessarily mean that the object is alien in any way. In fact, for some, the idea of the UFO is entirely unrelated to the search for alien life forms. Instead of looking towards the debris that might have crash landed on Earth, others decide to look upwards, towards the stars themselves when pondering the existence of intelligent extraterrestrial life forms. An excellent example of this comes from the life of Frank Drake, a radio astronomer from America who coined the now infamous Drake Equation.

At the time, Drake was working as part of the National Radio Astronomy Observatory stationed in West Virginia. During the early parts of 1960s, the concept of life beyond our own planet was seen as a joke by many scientists. But to Drake, the concept seemed to be a very real possibility. With a growing seriousness about the search for such life in the universe, he began to use his scientific background to demonstrate the likelihood of intelligent life forms existing beyond our comprehension. This became known as the Drake Equation, and it works like this:

The number of advanced technical civilizations in our galaxy (the Milky Way) will be labelled "N." If we want to find out the value of N, then we will need to know the following:

- R – How many stars in our galaxy are born each year?
- p – Of these stars, how many are orbited by planets?
- e – Of these planets, how many would be considered habitable?
- l – Life appears on how many of these planets?
- i – The life on how many of these planets has evolved to the point of intelligence?
- c – How many of these intelligent races can communicate with worlds other than their own?
- L – What is the average life of the civilizations in question?

When assembled, the Drake equation looks like this:

$$N = R.p.e.l.i.c.L$$

So, when we have the values of the information that we require, we can multiply them to find out the value of N, which is the number of intelligent civilizations that exist in the Milky Way. Of course, because the estimates for the values differs so much, the value can range from one to millions. This means that we might well be alone in the galaxy or surrounded by other civilizations searching for similar signs of intelligent life. Even then, the Drake Equation only investigates the Milky Way. As far as we know, there are 125 billion other galaxies in the universe. With numbers so ridiculously high, it is no wonder that many people see the question of there being intelligent life in the universe not as a yes/no response, but one of how many. Accordingly, if this number is so high, then is it that unfathomable that such a civilization might have paid a visit to our own planet? In doing so, might they have crash landed at sites such as Roswell or Tunguska? As one pulls back from the planet and starts to comprehend the sheer size of the universe, the chances that alien lifeforms might have been involved in some fashion does become – if not likely – then certainly more credible.

Laser Focus

Despite the large amount of focus on the possibility of alien life forms being behind the Tunguska Event, there were other theories circling around Russian literary groups. The science fiction writers had been behind much of the UFO speculation, but two other writers put forward another suggestion. It might seem strange that so much of the theorizing was dictated by authors, but in a state where the press was so heavily regulated and controlled, it was material published under the guise of fiction that so often was allowed to probe areas and ideas that the mainstream was not. The alternative theory put forward concerned the existence of a laser.

As per the theory, the Tunguska Event was the result of a misfiring intergalactic laser. Used by extraterrestrial life in order to try and determine more about the rest of the universe, the blast that hit the Siberian wilderness was a mistakenly aimed flurry of fire, possibly originating from a planet known to be orbiting around the star 61 Cygni, which can be found eleven light years from our own planet. The two authors who outlined the theory, Valentina Zhuravleva and Genrikh Altov, published their thoughts in the Zvezda magazine in 1964. As evidence, they pointed towards the eruption of Krakatoa as being an event that sent major shockwaves through the galaxy. Received in deep space eleven years later, it was mistaken as a means of greeting by distant alien scientists.

Then, the authors speculate, the alien scientists wished to respond. Following their customs, they decided to send back a message in a similar fashion. Being as their technology was much more advanced than what they perceived we possessed, they pointed a laser towards Earth. However, they misjudged the situation. Incorrectly entering the Earth's position, they shot the incredibly powerful laser through the universe, blasting an isolated region of Siberia. The people closest to the explosion, the Evenki community, did not have technology advanced enough to even guess at the meaning behind the laser blast and were thus unable to decode the message as it appeared to them.

Key to the theory is the Krakatoa signal. One of the first questions that the writers faced was just how could a volcano send a radio message? To this, they responded that the eruption flooded the atmosphere with a huge amount of volcanic ash. When entering into the atmosphere this caused a huge reaction, disturbing the ionosphere to the point where it caused the spontaneous creation of radio waves. So strong was the reaction that the waves exited out our galaxy and found their way to 61 Cygni. Even the selection of planet was justified; 61 Cygni is a binary star, one of only two stars that was known (in 1964) to possess an extra-solar planet. Though we now know that these kinds of planets can be fairly common, the Soviet writers were very deliberate in their selection. We also now know just how possible it can be to use lasers to communicate over huge interstellar distances.

The idea of intergalactic radio signals was also important. Drake himself was already using radio waves to send out messages into space. Named Project Ozma, he was using a radio telescope that measured twenty-six meters across to beam messages into the night. Specifically, he pointed his instruments towards Epsilon Eridani and Tau Ceti, both of which are eleven light years from Earth. Then he sat and listened, tuned into the frequency of one-and-one-half gigahertz, which is the same frequency as emitted by hydrogen gas, the most common element to be found across the whole universe. Though that yielded nothing, he was not dismayed. Similar radio wave emissions have been an almost constant feature of the space observing community ever since. But trying to find a response is incredibly tough. When it becomes clear just how large space is, trying to hit a distant planet with a specific radio signal is like trying to thread the world's tiniest needle. It might simply be that we are sending messages to the wrong place. As such, many people have suggested that an intergalactic laser would an ideal alternative.

The idea of sending a laser to communicate has two big advantages over trying to communicate using the incredible range of radio frequencies that are available. First, it is much easier to focus light into a single beam than it is with radio waves. This means that it is easier to focus the message on one target. Second, because the beam is so much more tightly focused, it's possible to pack a lot more information into a single communication. While we might be able to ask whether there's anyone there using radio waves, we can provide a full break down of our existence using a laser. However, there is a downside. Lasers are much more expensive when compared to radio waves and require a lot more power, a figure up in the billions of kilowatts. And that's just to broadcast for a miniscule amount of time. As laser technology gets cheaper and more advanced, the possibility of sending out more and more information grows. But if we have already accidently communicated with a civilization much more advanced than our own, then it stands to reason that they might have a much more refined understanding of laser technology. Could they then have pointed their laser at our planet and then made a simple mistake? While it remains unlikely, the remotest possibility exists that the Soviet authors might have uncovered the truth behind the mystery.

A Radioactive Environment

By 1969, interest in the Tunguska Event had moved outside of Russia. An American writer named George St. George was one of these men, as demonstrated by his book *Siberia: The New Frontier*. George had spent a large portion of his childhood in the remote Russia region and knew it well. In the book, he recounts tales of travelling through Siberia, a narrative that includes a mention of Tunguska. In the text, he touches upon the various theories that existed at the time. That is to say, he mentions the notion that the cause of the explosion might have been intelligently piloted due to the change in direction. When raising the possibility of whether this might be a confirmation of the existence of alien life or UFOs, he quotes the Russian Felix Zigel. In addition, he ranks the Tunguska Event among the highest echelons of alien-orientated events of interest for those serious about UFO investigations.

His stories go further. He recalls a time – in 1914 – when he talked about the matter when he was staying in the town of Chita. The conversation occurred between his father and a doctor friend, one who had mentioned the fact that he had been to the site of the explosion and seen the destruction for himself just a few months after the event. As proof, the doctor possessed a detailed diagram showing the course of the flight as it supposedly changed direction in the sky, moving over the course of at least a hundred miles. For weeks after the explosion, the locals said, there was a strange glow over the site. This suggested radiation. George's father was fascinated by the possibility of alien life forms and tied their existence to the local legends that recalled similar events. George's father suggested that they might be using Tunguska as a base of operations. Unfortunately, all of his writings and research were lost when the man died in 1928 while at a Buddhist monastery.

Perhaps what makes George St. George's account so interesting is the idea that someone visited the site in 1914. Apart from the Evenki, who did little to document any time they spent on the site, the first official visit to the site occurred with Leonid Kulik in 1927. It also demonstrates that even before the Bolshevik Revolution there were rumors, legends, and interest in the UFO folklore in Russia. The Russians were just as interested in the possibility of extraterrestrial life as many Americans are these days. Furthermore, George notes that there had been no documented radiation at the site at this point and speculates as to whether the site of the Tunguska Event might one day be as famous and popular among tourists as the huge meteor crater in Arizona. But the fact that he took time to note the lack of radiation demonstrates how much of a point of interest this was to everyone in the 1960s, in the midst of the Cold War.

One of the main proponents of the possibility of radioactive activity at the site of the Tunguska Event was Aleksei Zolotov, a geophysicist. Something of a mystery himself, Zolotov was once described by Moscow Radio as being "another noted investigator," though the scientific journal Nature painted a different portrait. The journal noted that his name occurred with regularity among any investigations into the Tunguska Event, even at the times when his theories and suggestions seemed patently outlandish. They noted the obscure nature of Zolotov's academic history, and there was even the suggestion that he had started life as an oil technician rather than as a scientist. It took ten years and twelve Zolotov-led expeditions to the site for the journal to finally relent and refer to him as something of an "authority in his own right."

But few have been so quick to dismiss the theories that Zolotov put forward. One of the main suggestions he had provided concerns atomic theory. According to him, the exploding spaceship as envisioned by Kazantsev held some water, though it was not actually an accident. As head of a Soviet research team in 1975, Zolotov was a key figure in the ongoing study of the Tunguska Event. At one point, he put forward the theory that aliens might well have purposefully detonated their own spaceship simply as a means of communicating their existence. Rather than a freak accident in an isolated region, the explosion was an impressive display of power, committed with "pinpoint accuracy and humanitarianism."

This idea of a humanitarian effort was expounded upon by T. R. LeMair, an American science writer. Published in 1980, he put forward the idea in his book entitled *Stones from the Stars*. By his reckoning, the timing of the Tunguska Event was too convenient to be a coincidence or an accident. Had it arrived a short time before or after, then the loss of life and infrastructure would have been huge. Had it arrived just slightly off course, then it might have crashed into an equally populated area. China, India, Moscow, and Korea would all have been within the realm of possibilities. Instead, LeMair posited, the object was being flown by a well-meaning pilot. The direction changes reflect a predetermined flight plan that landed the explosion just at the perfect point. This is contradicted by many eyewitness accounts, however, which neglect to mention any changes in course.

But the real lasting legacy of Zolotov's investigations into the Tunguska Event are focused on the radioactive nature of the explosion site. Often, he had been accused of simply lending scientific language and backing to the theories put forward by Kazantsev. Just as the writer built on the images from Nagasaki and Hiroshima, such as the mushroom cloud and the fireball, Zolotov concerned himself with the aftereffects. According to Zolotov, those who "survived" the Tunguska Event were hit by a heavy dose of radiation and suffered in a similar manner to those affected by the aftermath of the atomic bombs.

As if winning over support from other Tunguska theorizers, Zolotov found himself with the support of Zigel, who took to "Znanyie Sila" magazine to discuss his comrade's findings. Of chief concern were the expeditions that Zolotov had led in the three years before 1959. During these trips, one of the things studied had been the effects wrought by the ballistic waves from the so-called Tunguska body as it hung in the atmosphere, as well as the blast waves that had been created by the actual explosion. By studying the trees that had been left standing, Zolotov found that the ballistic waves had come first from a western direction and were only able to break the smaller branches. However, the blast from the north had been much stronger and had been able to break even the bigger tree limbs. His conclusion was that the blast waves had caused most of the destruction seen on the site.

When travelling up to 17 kilometers from the center of the blast, Zolotov found that the trees had been subjected to a high enough temperature that they had begun to burn. Ruling out the possibility of a natural forest fire, he placed his estimate for the size of the blast at about three and a half megatons. A blast of this size, he reasoned, would have to be nuclear.

The theory was not that outlandish. Soon, there seemed to be enough supporting evidence to lend it a lot more credence. Reindeer who had been in the area and who had survived were seen with mysterious scabs on their skin. The trees near the site, when felled, showed via their rings that they had experienced a massive increase in growth rate. There were high levels of carbon-14 (radioactive) in both the peat and the soil that the team collected from the area. All this and more pointed towards an abundance of radioactivity on the scene and that the blast had indeed been nuclear.

Aside from the aftermath of the bombs at Nagasaki and Hiroshima, there are traces of radioactivity around us at all times. There are traces of it in the soil under our feet and in the food we eat, as well as in the air, the water, and everything else that surrounds us. It's simply background radiation, and we receive a small dose of it every day. Usually, this can range from one and a half to three and a half millisieverts per year. Usually, the majority comes from food, drink, and other normal objects. But as much as twenty percent can come to us from artificial sources of radiation such as X-ray machines. Those who were able to survive Nagasaki and Hiroshima were, when studied, shown to have been exposed to many thousands of times more radiation in one moment than most people receive in an entire year. Furthermore, the radiation stayed at the bomb sites for a long time.

It was this kind of massive background radiation that was the focus of a lot of investigations in the 1950s and 1960s. A body known as the KSE (In English, The Interdisciplinary Independent Tunguska Expedition) was formed to investigate effects such as these. It made a start by studying the soil that was brought back from some expeditions. These scientists were based in Tomsk in Siberia, and it was joked that they were primarily tasked with disproving the spaceship theories that had started to form in the minds of many Russians.

One of their investigations involved looking into the effects of post-radiation illness that might be present in the Evenki people. A group of medical students led by KSE members collected data from those who lived near the Tunguska area but were not able to find any traces of the illness among any of the people. They even looked into the bones of the dead, people who had passed away since the explosion. This was difficult as the Evenki were very reluctant to tell people where these bodies were buried and did not want the graves disturbed. But the team managed to track down the remains of some people who had died during a 1915 smallpox epidemic, and these too showed no signs of illness related to exposure to massive amounts of radiation.

From the site, scientists were able to collect around 100 plant samples and 300 soil samples. These were analyzed in the KSE labs in Tomsk. It was found that there was between one and a half and two times higher levels of radiation in the samples collected from the epicenter of the blast when compared to soil from 40 kilometers away. However, they refused to comment on what might have caused this.

Another test was to compare the reports of the bright lights that had been seen around the world in 1908 with any reports that they could gather from the aftermath of American atomic test sites. The United States was regularly exploding atomic devices in Bikini Atoll by this time, and the scientists found that there were similar reports of lights in the sky following the detonation of nuclear devices. While it might not have been evidence that there had been a spaceship presence, many of the findings of KSE did point towards the possibility that there might have been a nuclear or radioactive element to the explosion that was previously not considered.

By the 1960s, there was a clear divide in the Russian scientific community on what might have caused the explosion. For two scientists in particular, the idea of a comet causing the Tunguska Event was much more likely. Vassilii Fesenkov and Kirill Florenskiy set out to prove that their comet theory was more correct that Zolotov's nuclear theory, with one of their key arguments being that there were simply no planets from which such a ship might have originated. In an interview with the New York Times in 1960, Fesenkov mentioned that the majority of the Russian scientists had now rejected the theory put forward by Zolotov.

Nevertheless, Florenskiy spent a lot of time between 1961 and 1962 trying to disprove the nuclear theories. According to his research, the levels of radiation that are found at the site of the explosion are well within the limits of normal fluctuation that you might find. He did admit that the average level of radiation was higher. His theory, however, was that the highest traces of radioactivity could be attributed to nuclear tests (conducted by humanity) that had somehow gotten into the soil and peat in the area. When asked to comment on the accelerated growth rate in trees, he commented that this was in line with the increase in growth that one normally sees in the wake of a large fire.

As recently as 2001, there have been further attempts to look into the matter of radioactive levels in the area. Nikolai Vasilyev, an academic, stated categorically that the results of investigations "negate a nuclear hypothesis." Critics in turn have pointed out that searching for such traces more than a century later can be almost impossible, especially when factoring in any contamination that might have been caused by Russian nuclear testing.

There are other indications that there may have been nuclear activity on the day of the Tunguska Event. Back in 1959, there were a number of graphs produced that seem to show that a magnetic storm took place in the hours following the Tunguska Event. Not typical of the aftermath of a meteor strike, such storms have been recorded in the wake of nuclear detonations. The geomagnetic field is disturbed by the detonation and can cause events that are very similar to the magnetic storms described.

The idea of a spaceship exploding over Tunguska will not go away. Some have even taken it further, suggesting that there might have been a battle between two separate spacecraft on that day, only one of which survived. Others have put forward the theory that a spaceship might have collided with a comet, neatly encompassing two competing suggestions and managing to satisfy almost no one. But even if the stories of the spaceship seem far-fetched and hard to believe, it is much harder to deny the existence of the traces of radiation that have been linked to the site. Looking into these levels of radioactivity could well be the best insight we have into uncovering exactly what happened that day, if only for the reason that they complicate the theory about a meteorite. If all of the information does not fit any one theory, then it might simply be that we do not have the right theory yet. However, the levels of radiation have led to one additional strange suggestion. Rather than a spaceship or a comet, might it have been an extraordinarily powerful weapon that caused the blast? And if so, who could possibly have invented such a device?

The Tesla Death Ray

The name Nikola Tesla might be familiar. There are people who have no idea who he is and people who claim that he should be remembered as one of the best and most important scientific minds of the last 500 years. According to his fans, he was so far ahead of his peers that even they failed to comprehend the importance of his inventions. In his obituary, the New York Times compared his abilities as an inventor to something befitting a Jules Verne novel, while reiterating his status as a genius in a time when the word might be overused.

Tesla was a ridiculously intelligent man. Dedicated to physics and mathematics, he would often conjure up blueprints for new creations that, though plausible, were beyond the capabilities of the resources that he had at his disposal. For many of his inventions, he still needed the world to catch up to his genius. But it was a misunderstood genius. Often considered a mad and renegade intelligence, he took on the mantle of a mad scientist for many people. It is said that the Superman cartoons from the forties created a mad scientist character when Max Fleischer, the creator of Superman, learned more about Tesla and his eccentric personality.

Alongside Thomas Edison, he was the epitome of the rush of invention that came at the tail end of the 19th Century and the early 20th Century. His list of inventions and discoveries includes AC power, dynamos, condensers, transformers, induction motors, mechanical rev counters, bladeless turbines, speedometers for automobiles, gas discharge lamps, broadcast radio, and 700 other patents that were filed with his name attached. His output was extraordinary and includes many inventions that we still take for granted today.

But as a man, he was not as comfortable with society as he was with science. An eccentric man, he ended his life as a recluse who sealed himself away from the rest of the world. He had no really close relationships during the course of his life and certainly was never married. Whenever he interacted with anyone, he insisted that they stand more than three feet away. During his final days, he was living out of a hotel room in New York where he kept pet pigeons. According to some people, Tesla essentially invented the Twentieth Century as we know it. But following his death in 1943, he faded into obscurity.

His name was revived somewhat in 1956, when scientists marked the centenary of his birth by naming a measuring unit for magnetism after him (a tesla is the SI unit for the density of magnetic flux). With a unit named after him, he has been raised into the illustrious company of Ampere, Ohm, Faraday, Hertz, and Volta. Added to this, the rise of the Internet has seen more and more people learning about the story of Nikola Tesla. Many websites and online portals have been dedicated to his memory, with there being a concerted effort to popularize the name of the man who invented so much. However, part of his appeal in the online world is at least partly due to some of his stranger theories and inventions. Among UFO fanatics and their ilk, Tesla's work on anti-gravity machines and free-energy has made him a cult figure. But there's one invention that stands out from his incredible portfolio, one that has been linked time and time again to the Tunguska Event: the Tesla death ray.

Nikola Tesla was a Croatian, born in 1856 on the 10th of July. He was the son of a Greek priest whose mother was a known inventor of appliances for the home and the farm. The son followed in his mother's footsteps, graduating high school to study engineering at a university. After completing his studies, he moved to New York at the age of 28. At the time, he was almost destitute. Aside from four cents in his hands, he had only a few scribbled drawings and outlines for a flying saucer he had dreamed up. He would spend the next sixty years living and working in New York, but he would die in almost the same situation as his arrival. At the time of his death, he had barely a penny to his name. But the scientific papers, research, blueprints, outlines, and sketches he left behind in his hotel room were incredible. Filled with ideas described as "revolutionary," the ideas were so far ahead of their time that we're only just managing to reinvent his ideas today. One such example is the Star Wars defense mechanism, a means of shooting down missiles in the air. Ostensibly conceived in the 1980s, there are plans for a remarkably similar system among Tesla's notes.

Tesla created the more practical of his inventions between 1886 and 1903. After that, it was a science fiction future that seemed to seduce him. After reading Jules Verne, the inventor became focused on ideas such as sending communications to Mars, using units of heat from the atmosphere to power engines, turning the entire planet into an electrical resonator so that people could instantly communicate from opposite sides of the Earth, and transmitting power through the cold, dark recesses of space. The last forty years of his life were dedicated to these high-flying and ultimately unprofitable ideas.

During these later years, Tesla was an easy target for any reporter who wanted a story on the supposed mad scientist. When he was 78, he gave one interview to a New York Times journalist who brought up some of the inventor's more deadly creations. In their discussion, Tesla happened to mention his plans for a death ray, a device so powerful that it might be able to destroy an entire army with one shot. A million soldiers would perish instantly from 250 miles away. The device could kill without a trace, the article told the readers, but assured them that the inventor saw the weapon as a defensive precaution only. According to Tesla's view, the death ray would simply make war an impossible venture. Leaving no marks beyond the destruction it caused, the device would surround a country and make it impenetrable to an air force or an invading army. But he never revealed the blueprints for such a device.

On his 84th birthday, Tesla returned to a similar idea. This time, he released a declaration stating that he was prepared to co-operate with the government on the idea of "teleforce." According to the scientist, this would allow the United States to instantly melt the motors in airplanes up to 400 kilometers away. This, too, would provide an impenetrable defense for the country and make it immune to the threat of invasion. Apparently, the teleforce operated by the means of a single beam that was focused to a diameter just one hundred millionth of a centimeter squared. All that was needed was a power source capable of supplying fifty million volts. The idea was dismissed as the ramblings of an old man and simply added to the pile of notorious inventions Tesla claimed to have foreseen. No one bothered to check the finer details.

But the idea for such a death ray probably had some pedigree. In 1902, the scientist set up a tower in Long Island measuring 57 meters in height. Surrounded by laboratories, it allowed him to conduct research on radio waves and the ways in which he could transmit electricity without the need for wires. The steel shaft of the tower plunged 36 meters into the ground but was topped with a huge metal dome weighing 55 tons and measuring 20 meters across. To fund this facility, Tesla had managed to secure the support of J. P. Morgan. However, before construction had even been finalized, the backer pulled out. Nine years later, Tesla had to abandon his incomplete tower and six years after that, it was demolished.

But there were reports that Tesla had managed to test his astonishing death ray regardless. According to the legend, it was a night in 1908, and an explorer named Robert Peart was in the Arctic making another attempt to find the North Pole. He had been talking to Tesla beforehand and had received a strange request from the scientist. When he was near the Arctic, Tesla had said, he should look up to the sky and see if he noticed anything unusual. On the 30th of June, Tesla was in his tower. He switched on the machines at his disposal and pointed everything towards the north, supposedly just to the west of where he assumed Peary was stationed. During the next few days, he scanned the newspapers for any mention of Peary and requested telegrams daily from the explorer, wondering whether he had seen anything. But there was no response of note. Nothing seemed to have happened in the Arctic. But reports of another kind began to filter through. In the coming days, Tesla learned more and more about a strange explosion in Siberia. Though details were thin on the ground, the scientist seemed to have known better. Quietly, he began to dismantle the tower he had built and took apart every single piece, pleased that no one had been hurt by his efforts. It seemed to him that the device was simply too dangerous to be allowed to exist.

In the months leading up to this, Tesla had been in correspondence with the New York Times. Writing a letter to the newspaper, he detailed what he meant when he referred to the idea of "future warfare." In his opinion, it would be conducted by using the "direct application of electrical waves." There would be no need for planes, tanks, or troops. According to his vision, the potential of wireless power meant that it was easy to make any place on the planet uninhabitable without the need to subject

68

the local people to any danger or even any inconvenience. The idea was that, with a machine so incredibly powerful, the very idea of war would be abandoned as futile. It was a commendable philosophy, but it revealed the naïve nature of some of Tesla's thinking when it came to humanity. As disproved following the invention of the atomic bomb, the world had never been closer to self-destruction than when it was in possession of the means to instantly wipe out life on the planet. So while it seems as though Tesla's intentions for a death ray might have aligned with the destruction seen during the Tunguska Event, there remains doubts.

First, there is no evidence that Tesla was able to use his tower for his experiments on the death ray machine. By 1908, he had lost the majority of his funding, something that would certainly be needed if only to power the device. Second, it seems as though there is a desire to link two of the early Twentieth Century's strangest and most alluring concepts: the Tunguska Event and Nikola Tesla. While they might appear to be well-matched, it can often come down to wishful thinking on behalf of the scientist's fan base. Third, there is no proof that Tesla's supposed death ray was ever anything more than a pipedream. The loss of his papers and blueprints after his death means that we may never know what he was working on when he died.

But that's not to say that some people don't support the theory of Tesla somehow being involved in or at the very least, certainly being capable of inventing a device like the death ray. The idea definitely chimes with his own feelings. A book was released in 1908 titled *Wireless Technology and Telephony*. In the text, writers Massie and Underhill talk to Tesla about his idea of how radio waves might be used in the future. According to the scientist, his experiments would make it possible for a man in New York to instantly communicate instruction to a man in London. While the telephone at the time was a nascent venture, Tesla already envisioned a future where it was possible to sit at one's desk, look up the phone number of anyone on the planet, and get in touch with them immediately without the need for special equipment. All they needed was a device roughly the size of a watch. That same device would allow them to tune into any form of broadcast, from music to sermons to political speeches. They could even transmit drawings or images around the planet, all made possible thanks to wireless technology. At the time it was pure science fiction. Now the technology is so commonplace that we take it for granted.

So there is no doubt that Tesla had a better handle of the potential for radio waves and wireless power than most of his peers. As he promised at the time, people might be doubtful, but his experiments would soon leave them assured of his convictions. Though he never completed the tower that housed his experiments, he never gave up on the dream. He wrote at least one letter to J. P. Morgan asking him to reconsider the decision to pull out of the venture. In the letter, he promised that he already "perfected" the technology, which he described as the "greatest of our time." This work was focused on the transmission of energy from one place to another without the need for wires. It hints towards the possibility of a machine such as the death ray, but there is very little as to how such a weapon might work. The closest we come to an explanation arrived much later, in 1937, when Tesla wrote an article about projecting "concentrated non-dispersive energy" through what he named the "natural media." The piece is highly technical and impenetrable to those without a decent understanding of electricity and how it might be transmitted. But taking a step back from the minute details, it is possible to see how technology might be applied to a device like the legendary death ray.

Tesla's death ray exists more as a speculative thought experiment rather than an actual piece of working technology. As far as we know, there was never a prototype. Tesla was never allowed the chance to construct the device as he envisioned it. But there are more holes in the story that such a weapon might have been the true cause of the Tunguska Event. Despite the claims made by people who buy into the argument, it is unlikely that Tesla could ever have learned about the Tunguska Event before 1928, long after his tower was demolished. Before then, the stories in the American newspapers were limited to recollections of strange lights in the sky, rather than an explosion in Siberia. Similarly, the accounts of the explorer Peary don't mention Tesla by name, and it seems as though many people place him into the story simple by joining together the sparse facts of the case. Added to this, Tesla's noted pacifism seems to be at odds with the creation of such a high-powered weapon. While he might have seen it as a way of stopping wars, he would be utterly naïve to think that it might never be used on a human population. According to proponents of the theory, however, Tesla might have intended the demonstration as a publicity event that would hurt no one and simply got it wrong.

There are many conspiracy theories attributed to Nikola Tesla. The man is undoubtedly compelling. There have been suggestions that following his death, the government was the first to arrive at his hotel room, and they left with their choice pick of his most interesting inventions, which might have included the plans for a giant death ray. His work on energy and radio waves was revolutionary and incredibly far ahead of his time, and if one desires, the Tunguska Event can be made to fit the profile of a testing site for a new weapon of untold destructive prowess. But as with many aspects of Tesla's life, the theory relies too much on speculation. Though the Tunguska Event only plays a role in the story of one of the world's most interesting men, trying to solve the mystery of the explosion in Siberia must instead turn to the possibilities that can be proven. As Tesla himself would no doubt demand, there much be evidence, results, and scientific method when attempting to explain the inexplicable. If the stranger theories are perhaps a little too strange, then what are the more concrete explanations for what happened during the Tunguska Event?

Finding the Answers

When examining the possible causes of the Tunguska Event, a recent poll undertaken in the Russian media can point us in the direction of the range of choices that are available. Sent out to a wide variety of people online, the poll asked each person what they felt was the specific cause of the explosion in Siberia on the 30th of June, 1908. The four options were: a comet; a meteorite/asteroid; an alien spacecraft; or other. While there might not be a definitive answer, and it is not backed up by scientific justifications, the fact that these are the four possible answers outlines the key theories that are available. But first, it might be time to pay more attention to the first two options, the possibility of whether a meteorite, asteroid, comet, or something similar struck the Siberian wilderness on that day.

At various points in this book, we have already touched upon the idea of a piece of space debris hurtling head first into the Earth and causing a massive explosion. The Chicxulub crater in Mexico, for example, is a place where a massive ball of rock and ice struck the planet with incredible power. There is a prevailing theory that such an event is what caused the mass extinction of the dinosaurs and that similar collisions have occurred at regular periods throughout the history of the planet. If it is the case that the Tunguska Event was caused by such a phenomena, then we might count ourselves lucky. Meteorite strikes such as the one that caused the Mexican crater can be utterly devastating on a planetary scale, and even though it was one of the most powerful explosions in recorded human history, we are fortunate that the Tunguska Event was a relatively minor blast.

But what exactly is the difference between comets, asteroids, meteors, and meteorites? To many, these seem to be interchangeable names from the same phenomena: huge rocks that fall to the Earth from space. But there are key differences that have been determined by scientists and will be needed before we continue.

Comet

Comets, along with asteroids, are believed to be ancient fragments of matter that date back as far as the formation of the solar system. These fragments can be billions of years old, time that they have spent moving around the "planetary neighborhood" in a manner very different to planets, moons, and stars. A comet is a body made up of rock, ice, and even organic compounds. They can measure several miles in diameter and are supposedly originally from the areas beyond the orbit of the planets in a solar system. They usually follow regular orbits, and this means that they can appear above us at timely intervals. One example is Haley's Comet, which appears near the Earth once every 75 years. Seen by many as balls of ice that hurtle through space, comets can occasionally be dragged from their path by gravitational fluctuations. They often have a tail that can be seen from our planet, a trail of debris that they leave behind in their wake. The impact of comets on our planet during its early years may have caused many of the geological formations we know today, such as oceans, mountains, and craters.

Asteroid

An asteroid is similar to a comet but with a number of key differences. Most are made from rocks, though there are some that are embedded with metals (typically iron and nickel). Their size can vary hugely, from being as big as a boulder to many hundreds of miles across. Some asteroids might be comets that have "burned out" and slowed down. The majority of asteroids can be found in the asteroid belts, one of which orbits between Mars and Jupiter. They are locked into an orbit and sometimes come very close to our own planet. There is a history of asteroids crashing into Earth, leaving behind massive craters and wiping out huge amounts of life. These strikes can destroy the planet or an area surrounding the crash zone but are thankfully very rare.

Meteoroid

If "asteroid" is the name given to the larger bodies that orbit around the sun, then "meteoroid" is the name given to the smaller equivalents. It is often a small particle or object that has detached from a comet or asteroid. A meteoroid has the possibility of becoming a meteor or a meteorite, a difference that is dictated by its behavior once it makes contact with the Earth's atmosphere.

Meteor

Sometimes referred to as a shooting star, a meteor is a meteoroid that has entered into the Earth's atmosphere and started to burn up. This vaporization is caused by the heat generated when entering into the Earth's atmosphere, as well as being affected by the velocity and the angle of entry. If a Meteoroid does enter our atmosphere, then typically the huge amount of heat that they are subjected to means that they will burn up and become meteors.

Meteorite

When a meteoroid enters into our atmosphere and does not immediately begin to disintegrate, then it becomes a meteorite. In order to take this title, it must come into connection with the surface of the Earth. It if burns up before it reaches the ground, then it remains as a regular meteor. Because they leave behind debris, meteorites are incredibly interesting to science. They can be pieces of space rock that have travelled far beyond the capabilities of our own technology, visiting parts of the galaxy that we might never hope to reach. It can even be possible, thanks to rigorous analysis, to determine the origin of the metal, tracking it back to its formation four and a half billion years ago. If you read about a meteoroid that enters into the atmosphere and has been recovered, then chances are that it will be a meteorite.

So, the question now remains, if the Tunguska Event was caused by one of the above, then which one might it have been and how can we tell? As per the results of the survey that was sent out to the Russian people, thirty-one percent said that they believed a comet to be the cause of the explosion. Twenty-seven percent attributed the Event to a meteorite or an asteroid. Only nine percent believed it to be the result of an alien spacecraft. Thirty-three percent, however, noted their opinion as other. As this final option leaves the possibilities wide open, the combined total of comet, asteroid, and meteorite seems to suggest that close to sixty percent of people believe that some kind of space debris was responsible for the explosion.

But this was a public poll. Even though it was hosted on a science-orientated Russian website, it is not the most rigorous way in which to determine the truth. While useful for an outline of the most widely believed theories, surely we must turn to the international science community for a peer-reviewed and singular answer? But there exists an equal divide among those who have studied the Tunguska Event in a professional capacity.

As such, Professor Chris Trayner of the University of Leeds put forward a theory that attempted to explain just why there was such as massive divide among scientists as to the cause of the Event. According to Trayner, the difference can be traced back to the Iron Curtain, the divide between East and West during the Cold War. During this time, there was a paucity of Russian literature and research available to those in the West. Without a huge amount of translated resources and source materials, scientists in the West were forced to study from afar, without first-hand access to the information. If there is ever to be an agreement on the cause of the Event, then these materials must be made available to scientists in the West, in order that they can better elaborate, expand upon, and refine the Russians' theories. But it goes both ways. There are a great many Western scientists who have managed to do good work on the Tunguska Event, so Trayner mentions that their findings must also be translated into Russian and made available to scientists in the East. The work of Chris Trayner points to just how complex it has been to try and establish a set of agreed-upon principles. As we try to pick apart the Tunguska Event, we should first define those talking points on which everyone is in agreement.

It seems that scientists are able to agree on the following:

1. The time of the Tunguska Event. There is little doubt that the time the explosion took place was 07:14am local time, with the epicenter of the event being traced to a specific latitude and longitude (60 degrees 55 minutes north, 101 degrees 57 minutes east respectively).
2. That a large object was spotted in the sky by people in the vicinity. Presumably, this object would be a comet or a meteorite, as it was spotted across an area of one and a half thousand square kilometers. According to witnesses, the object was comparable in brightness to the sun at midday.
3. The object exploded before it hit the ground. According to the witness reports, the explosion occurred roughly five to ten kilometers from the surface. This explosion, it is agreed, then generated a massive amount of power, probably between ten and twenty megatons.
4. Debris from the blast was hurled into the air and up into the stratosphere. Despite this, there have been no significant fragments recovered from anywhere other than the site itself and the relatively untouched Antarctica.
5. The force of the blast created a shockwave powerful enough to flatten over two thousand square kilometers of Siberian forest. Roughly two hundred square kilometers showed signs of being burned by an intense heat wave. While typical forest fires are known to burn the bottom parts of trees, these burn marks were seen continuously and uniformly along the entire tree.
6. Despite searches on numerous expeditions, no crater was found. The epicenter of the blast shows

no signs of an impact crater, created either by a collision with the Earth or where the explosive shock wave first hit the ground.

7. When examined from above, the area of the blast takes the shape of a butterfly. After examining the area, scientists believe that the epicenter of the blast took place at the so-called "head" of the butterfly.

8. Witnesses as far away as Vanavara (70 kilometers) were said to be able to feel the shock and heat waves in the aftermath of the explosion. Furthermore, bright lights were seen in the atmosphere as far away as 700 kilometers, while people 1,200 kilometers away reported hearing sounds at the time of the Event that they likened to gunfire.

9. The disturbances in the atmosphere that were created by the Event were felt around the planet. The generation of seismic waves was a phenomena that was not only felt in Russia, but could also be detected from other countries.

10. In the hours following the explosion, a large magnetic storm gathered over the blast site. Notably similar to the storms that are created in the aftermath of atmospheric nuclear detonations, it began shortly after the blast and continued for roughly four hours.

11. The Tunguska Event was the cause of the bright lights that were observed across Europe and Asia in the aftermath of the explosion. There was also the observation of noctilucent clouds. These sights were likely caused by the dust that was thrown into the atmosphere.

12. The trees that survived the blast were shown to exhibit a notable acceleration in their growth rates following the Event.

These twelve points provide the starting point for almost any researcher who wants to look into the Tunguska Event. Together, these facts represent the collected findings of more than one hundred years of interest and research. The difficulty in crossing language and cultural barriers in order to crack the case is made so much more challenging when the agreed-upon details can be surmised in less than a page. Because of this, it should be no shock to see that there exists such a massive difference in opinion as to what really happened, as well as there being a scope for many theories and suppositions that manipulate the appointed facts to suit particular ideas.

But just as there are points on which everyone can agree, there are also those that cause constant tension and disagreement between researchers. Whether this is because of the mistranslations and misunderstandings that are sure to crop up, it cannot be said. But there is also much furor about the following points among scientists within their own respective cultures and disciplines. So now that we know the designated points, what are the more contentious ideas?

1. The shape of the object that was seen in the sky has been described in many different ways. People have variously called it a tube, a pillar, and a pipe, while others have questioned whether it did in fact leave a trail of smoke or dust when travelling through the sky.

2. As well as the shape of the object, people have questioned its mass and nature, even going so far as to debate just how long it spent in the sky above Tunguska.

3. A major point of contention (and one that is difficult to prove) relates to the entry angle of the object and the flight path it took before exploding. Wrapped up in this question is the velocity of the object in question and just how long the explosion lasted once it started.

4. There are people who believe in a single explosion, and there are those who have said that there were multiple blasts on the day. As a counter theory, some people have suggested that there were echoes of the first blast that led to the illusion of multiple explosions.

5. Radioactivity around the blast site is constantly questioned. Scientists and researchers have long debated the genetic effects on both the local human and tree population, with the latter being said to demonstrate accelerated growth rates. Certain scientists have attributed this to radiation at the scene, while others say that it is a natural response to the burning down of nearby plant life and can be seen in trees that survive forest fires.

6. There are craters on the site, though there is still questions about whether they were in fact caused by the explosion. Though most now agree that there is no major crater, others have argued for the existence of multiple smaller craters such as the Suslov crater.

7. Some people have even questioned the existence of the optical anomalies that were seen in the sky after the event, claiming that similar effects can be accounted for as early as the 23rd of June, a full week before the Tunguska Event.

8. Finally, there have been suggestions that the object changed path in its flight a number of times. However, these have now been largely dismissed and very few people still adhere to this version of events.

With so many discrepancies among the theories put forward, it becomes clear just why there are so many competing theories out there. For example, there might be a widely established notion that the Event was caused by a comet or meteor, though which one of these and the manner in which it occurred still remain up for debate. Even within the main theories, there exist sub-theories and suggestions that scientists are more than happy to debate endlessly.

The Key Theories

With that in mind, it is now time to lay out the central arguments that have been put forward about the Tunguska Event. While many people favor the outlandish (and arguably more interesting) theories, the majority of the scientific community rallies behind one of the scenarios outlined below.

Gathering together the sheer range of theories about the Tunguska Event is tough, and due to issues of space, there are some that simply cannot be included in this book. As an example, P. I. Privalova constructed a list of the major theories in 1969. A Russian writer (whose real name was Igor Zotkin) interested in the Event, managed to gather together at least 77 different theories. In the near half-century between the publication of his list and now, there have been even more put forward. Some of these theories are so close as to be almost brothers, while others are so different as to be almost another species entirely. According to Privalova himself, the initial list of 77 could easily be stretched to over 120 if one were willing to sit down at a campfire and listen to stories over a bottle of vodka. However, for the purposes of this text, we will focus on the twelve main theories and the ones that are (rightly or wrongly) most often discussed among those most interested in the Tunguska Event.

1. **A disintegrating comet that entered our atmosphere**. It is alleged that a comet with an unusually loose composition entered into the Earth's atmosphere. As it entered, it began to break up and fall apart with ease. As it disintegrated, the nucleus of the comet was left at a size of around 40 meters (much smaller than the majority of comets) and this then exploded over Tunguska.

2. **An exploding asteroid**. This theory places the explosion of a 30-meter-wide asteroid at roughly eight kilometers in the air. In doing so, it released a blast amounting to around 15 megatons and resulted in a million tons of tiny particles being released into the world's atmosphere. This dust was then blown around by the winds and caused the bright lights to appear around the world.

3. **A miniature black hole visited Earth**. Though we have not touched upon the idea of a black hole in great depth, this theory proposes that an invisible black hole appeared first at the site of the explosion and then moved through the planet itself for roughly a quarter of an hour. It then exited through the Atlantic Ocean (on the other side of the world) and this exit causes shock waves to ripple through the atmosphere and the ocean.

4. **The annihilation of a rock of anti-matter was caused when it touched the regular matter of the Earth's atmosphere**. This event caused a blast measuring 35 megatons and generated many trillions of the carbon-14 atoms that we know to be radioactive.

5. **A rock made of "mirror matter" entered the atmosphere**. Also known as "shadow matter" or "Alice matter," mirror matter is a hypothetical opposite of our ordinary matter that differs from anti-matter. When a rock constructed of this material arrived in our atmosphere and contacted regular matter, it exploded. According to the theory, the mirror matter rock measured about 100 meters across and had a mass of around a million tons.

6. **A volcanic eruption**. This more familiar theory suggests that the escape of natural gas occurred through a number of narrow underground vents. These volcanic vents saw a huge amount of gas race through towards the surface at incredible speeds, whereupon it began to mix with the environment. After a number of hours, this created

a mixture of amazing volatility, amounting to around ten million tons of methane gas. This gas then exploded.

7. **Huge ball lightning that appeared from nowhere**. Ball lightning is still a mysterious natural phenomenon, but it has been suggested that a 200-meter- wide (or up to one kilometer) example materialized in Tunguska. It continuously broke up into a number of smaller balls and then into an even smaller selection of balls until they broke down and released a huge amount of energy.

8. **A phenomena named "geometeors" that appeared from within the Earth**. Our knowledge of the interior of the Earth is limited at best, and it has been suggested that the blast might have been caused by the bond between atmospheric and subterranean events. These events were able to form luminous objects with many of the same qualities as meteors. These then exploded when reaching the surface.

9. **A plasmoid from the Sun arriving at Earth**. It has been suggested that a plasmoid weighing 100,000 tons was expelled from the Sun. Lacking the technology to observe and understand space as we currently do, the people of 1908 were unprepared for the appearance of such a massive, unexpected plasmoid and had no word to describe it.

10. **A crashed alien spaceship**. One of the more commonly abandoned theories, the idea of an extraterrestrial ship that somehow broke down and

vaporized is nevertheless enduringly popular. Out of control, it is suggested that the destruction of the ship (and its power source) was the reason for the Tunguska Event.

11. **A mistaken communication with an alien laser**. After being heralded by the radio waves emitted by the eruption of Krakatoa, an alien planet attempted to beam a communication to Earth using a powerful laser. Whether it went wrong or the explosion was their intended effect, the theory splinters depending on the individual believer.

12. **A new super-weapon that was new released**. This is the theory that Nikola Tesla might have created a death ray and when testing it, realized the horrific potential of the weapon. Believers say he then dismantled it so that it could not fall into the wrong hands.

Though many of the theories start out with an increased amount of scientific integrity, many of the later attributions deteriorate into the more outlandish and strange. As you can imagine, some of the theories propose even stranger and more complicated explanations for the explosions, though these are commonly dismissed. So, now that we have an overview, do the twelve theories outlined above hold up too interrogation?

A Closer Look

When you begin to take a closer look at some of the theories on offer about the Tunguska Event, it becomes clear that some are far more credible than others. However, is there a single theory that is able to explain everything?

1. **A disintegrating comet that entered our atmosphere**. This remains the most popular theory among the Russian people. The evidence we have of the Tunguska Object's orbit remains in line with the orbits of asteroids but is not consistent with what we know about comets. Short-period comets (the type referred to in the theory) typically need a huge mass in order to survive entry into an atmosphere. For example, a comet named Shoemaker-Levy 9 crashed into Jupiter in recent years, and it was observed that comets would need to have a mass of more than a hundred million tons in order to remain intact during entry and trigger an explosion of the type seen in Siberia. It is estimated by some scientists that the mass of the object reportedly in the skies was as much as one million tons. A small comet of this size could not conceivably survive the pressures induced by entering into the atmosphere of our planet. Instead of a comet, the only object of this type that might have survived in a size big enough to have caused the explosion would be an asteroid.

2. **An exploding asteroid**. The evidence against it having been an asteroid come from the qualities of the object that are so like a comet. The object seemingly had a loose structure that caused it to break apart in the atmosphere. The dust trail that should be expected of a comet (but not an asteroid) would have been hidden by the sun, though it would still have managed to cause unusual sunsets. Similarly, no one was able to spot the comet before it arrived due to it arriving from the direction of the sun, the glare obscuring the object as it arrived. The absence of any recovered fragments of asteroids mean that the object must surely have been a comet.

3. **A miniature black hole visited Earth**. Though still young in scientific terms, our knowledge of black holes has increased rapidly over recent decades. While it does seem theoretically possible for a miniature black hole to pass through the Earth, the theory collapses when it becomes impossible to provide proof of said black hole exiting on the other side of the planet. Because of this, evidence seems to indicate that the object was a massive rock, rather than a black hole that no one could see.

4. **The annihilation of a rock of anti-matter was caused when it touched the regular matter of the Earth's atmosphere**. This theory is best dismissed when we turn to the idea that it would instantly have obliterated when coming into contact with the Earth's atmosphere, rather than four kilometers above Tunguska. The eyewitness

accounts and the way in which anti-matter and matter instantly annihilate discredit the theory.

5. **A rock made of "mirror matter" entered the atmosphere**. Similar to the above, this theory seems to fall apart when we look at eyewitness accounts. The object was not a rock, but it has been described as a ball.

6. **A volcanic eruption**. Looking at the radial manner in which the trees fell, it becomes apparent that the shockwaves came not from below, but rather from above. Also, the eyewitness accounts of a giant fireball moving across the sky seem to dismiss the idea that it could have emerged from a subterranean cavity.

7. **Huge ball lightning that appeared from nowhere**. As mentioned above, ball lightning is still little understood by science. However, there have been no other examples and no conceivable way in which ball lightning of any size could have converted into an explosion of the type seen in 1908.

8. **A phenomena named "geometeors" that appeared from within the Earth**. This theory has been easily dismissed by the majority of scientists as it seems to be based on a lack of hard evidence. Similarly, it is not known how an object could appear from within the Earth with enough velocity to cause the levels of destruction seen in Tunguska.

9. **A plasmoid arriving at Earth from the Sun**. A plasmoid is kind of like a vessel contained with plasma that surrounds itself with a sizeable magnetic field. However, they are uncommon on our planet, more of a theoretical idea than something we regularly observe, especially of the size and power that caused the explosion in question.

10. **A crashed alien spaceship**. The key to disproving or discrediting this theory lies in the lack of evidence. While technically a very, very remote possibility, it relies on manipulating the facts to suit the theory rather than gathering verifiable information that points directly at an answer.

11. **A mistaken communication with an alien laser**. Just as with the spaceship idea, this theory relies too heavily on supposition. In addition, though there might have been very limited choice of suitable planets at the time the theory was coined, recent research has revealed that there is a huge number of planets that share similar characteristics, none of which have previously attempted anything resembling communication.

12. **A new super-weapon that was new released**. The final theory seems to rely too heavily on the legend of Nikola Tesla. While certainly a fascinating figure, he left no examples of his death ray, not even plans or blueprints (though they could have been stolen by the US government). Similarly, the huge amount of power that would have been required to fire the machine would have been very costly and without a financial backer, it

is unlikely that Tesla could have raised the funds to test the death ray himself.

So where does that leave us? The majority of the theories have at least one glaring flaw that means the argument can be dismissed. To most people, the choice comes down to a decision between an asteroid and a comet, with recent years seeing an uptake in the number of people who are willing to back the stony asteroid theory. Whereas the comet used to dominate thoughts about the Tunguska Event, the asteroid alternative seems to offer many of the same qualities with fewer of the drawbacks.

But as we have seen, there are always new attempts to provide an answer. The asteroid theory has its flaws and without having any definitive evidence, can only ever remain a hypothesis. That is why there is an almost continuous effort to explain the destruction of Tunguska. Look at the recent black hole and mirror matter theories as an example. In the aftermath of the Tunguska Event, there was very little knowledge of such scientific areas. But as our knowledge of the galaxy and the universe has grown, we have found new theories that can be applied to previous events. As we search more and more, we may yet uncover more truths and previously unknown details about physics that help us arrive closer to an answer.

The Tunguska Event is important because it has remained a mystery for over a hundred years. Over the past century, people have attempted to provide hundreds of explanations for one of the most destructive events in the history of man. It has been described as a mystery and a miracle, it has become an obsession and an oddity. While the jury may remain out on the true nature of the explosion, there remains no doubt over the captivating nature of the Tunguska Event.

Conclusion

It might seem strange to arrive at the end of an investigation into the truth about the Tunguska Event and not find a concrete answer. While it remains likely that the explosion was caused by a stony asteroid entering the Earth's atmosphere and exploding four kilometers above the ground, there exists enough reasonable doubt so that it becomes impossible to provide an absolute answer. There are traces and clues that point toward other theories, while there are flaws that have been pointed out time and time again with the prevailing theories. If there is one thing that we know for sure about the cause of the Tunguska Event, it is that there is nothing that it 100% confirmable.

But perhaps this is where the true wonder of the awesome Event lies. Rather than attempting to unravel every thread and chase down every lead, there are times when we should simply sit back and wonder at the astonishing nature of the phenomena, all while noting just how lucky it was that the explosion occurred in the deep wilderness of Siberia. While it is the isolation, the strangeness, and the incredible power that most attract people to the mystery of the Tunguska Event, the exact same qualities likely mean that we will never be able to find the truth.

But there is a chance. As we have seen, the bulk of the theories have been devised, embellished, and often discredited many years after the initial Event. Whether you believe that there was a spaceship involved or whether you believe a mini black hole passed through the planet, all of these theories have been devised long after 1908. And this is what provides us with hope. As we uncover more information about the world around us and learn about our place in the universe, we will no doubt have newer ways in which to interpret the data. It might be that we discover some new type of cosmic event or that little grey men visit us and wonder why we never replied to their messages. At some point in the future, we might finally have the tools to uncover the truth. Until then, the Tunguska Event will remain one of the greatest (and least known) mysteries of human history.

Further Reading

Baxter, J. and Atkins, T. (1976). *The fire came by*. Garden City, N.Y.: Doubleday.

Bronshtėn, V. (2000). *Tungusskiĭ meteorit*. Moskva: A.D. Sel'ianov.

Furneaux, R. (1977). *The Tungus event*. New York: Nordon.

Gallant, R. (1995). *The day the sky split apart*. New York: Atheneum Books for Young Readers.

Rubtsov, V. (2009). *The Tunguska mystery*. New York: Springer.

Stoneley, J. and Lawton, A. (1977). *Cauldron of hell*. New York: Simon and Schuster.

Image Credits

1. Map showing the approximate location of the Tunguska event of 1908. This is a hacked version of the public domain map Russia-CIA WFB Map.png. User:Bobby D. Bryant made the modifications and uploaded it under the GFDL on May 21, 2005.

2. Photograph from Kulik's 1929 expedition taken near the Hushmo River. ru:Евгений Леонидович Кринов, member of the expedition to the Tunguska event in 1929.

3. Still taken from raw footage from the 1921 Tunguska expedition showing the aftermath of the huge Tunguska explosion in 1908.

4. Leonid Kulik By Евгений Леонидович Кринов, a member of the expedition to the site of the Tunguska event. - http://omzg.sscc.ru/tunguska/photos/kulik.html, Public Domain, https://commons.wikimedia.org/w/index.php?curid =3037057

About the Author

Conrad Bauer is passionate about everything paranormal, unexplained, mysterious, and terrifying. It comes from his childhood and the famous stories his grandfather used to tell the family during summer vacation camping trips. He vividly remembers his grandfather sitting around the fire with new stories to tell everyone who would gather around and listen. His favorites were about the paranormal, including ghost stories, haunted houses, strange places, and paranormal occurrences.

Bauer is an adventurous traveler who has gone to many places in search of the unexplained and paranormal. He has been researching the paranormal and what scares people for more than four decades. He also loves to dig into period of history that are still full of mysteries, being an avid reader of the mystic secret societies that have mark history and remain fascinating and legendary throughout the times. He has accumulated a solid expertise and knowledge that he now shares through his books with his readers and followers.

Conrad, now retired, lives in the countryside in Ireland with his wife and two dogs.

More Books from Conrad Bauer

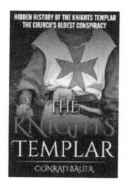 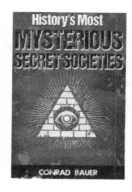 

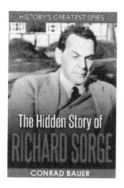 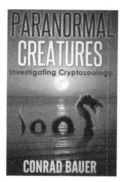 

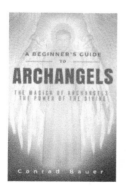  

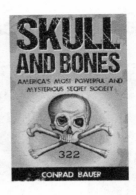

Made in the USA
Monee, IL
14 July 2021

73637150R00062